SUCCESS STORIES
of a
FAILURE ANALYST

THE LIFE OF FRANKLIN ST. JOHN

GREG OLEAR

Bottom line, you're either a risk taker or you're not, and if you don't take risks, you'll never win big.

—Geno Auriemma

For Sam, C.J., Henry, Dominick, and Milo

CONTENTS

PART THREE: PENNSYLVANIA

PART FOUR: WALLINGFORD

PART FIVE: CHINA & BEYOND

PREFACE

Frankie St. John in front of a neighbor's house,
L'Anse, Michigan, ca. 1948.

MY FATHER-IN-LAW WAS BORN IN 1938, in a house without a toilet, in a flyspeck of a town in the Upper Peninsula of Michigan. His grandfathers were both lumberjacks. His father was a plowman. If anything was expected of Franklin St. John at all, it was that he would follow one of those two career paths. Instead, through more quirks of fate that can quickly be recounted, he became, of all things, a metallurgical engineer.

In his colorful early career—colorful for an engineer, that is—he encountered transplanted Nazi scientists, crooked cops on the make, and mobbed-up steel plant managers. At the height of the Vietnam War, he worked for a company that made engines and propellers for army helicopters. As a failure analyst—an industrial job that kept him far away from the jungles of Indochina—Frank identified and fixed a manufacturing problem that had led to helicopter engines failing on the battlefield, saving the lives of untold number of soldiers.

When he was 40 years old, he invented an alloy called "unit bond," specially engineered to adhere to porcelain—most metals don't—and intended to be used as a substitute for gold in the manufacture of dental bridges and crowns. Unit bond cost 40 cents an ounce to make. He sold it for $16.95 per ounce. Customers ordered hundreds of ounces at a time. When he cashed out ten years later, Frank was worth something like $18 million—and he was still bringing home $300,000 a year, guaranteed, as part of his buyout agreement.

He gave away the lion's share of his fortune, mostly to his alma mater, Michigan Tech. It is no stretch to say that he has helped thousands of students pay for their schooling. ("Schooling" is a word he uses a lot). He retired at age 50, traveled the world from Hong Kong to Vatican City to Antarctica, and became obsessed with the UConn Women's basketball team.

Through it all, Frank seemed always to know when to stay and when to leave. At all times, he seemed to have, as he put it, a "sixth sense" about how to handle certain situations and what to do next—almost like his guardian angel was top of its class.

Although wealthy, Frank is not extravagant. He owns a Lexus, but he lives in the same Cape Cod house in the same middle-class Connecticut town where my wife grew up. When I first visited him there 22 years ago, he was sitting in a den built out of the breezeway between the garage and the house proper, bundled in blankets because there was no heat in there, watching the UConn game on a crappy console TV. But he does enjoy the ancillary benefits that his wealth confers. He likes to overtip. He likes to randomly buy his loved ones gifts. After his father died, he flew back to the Upper Peninsula and, in 24 hours, negotiated and closed on a new lot for his mother to build a house; he paid cash. He once put ten grand in a shoebox and mailed it to his sister in Michigan.

Franklin is a storyteller, like his father and grandfather before him. Over the last few years, he wrote down a lot of his stories, recalled in a folksy and endearing style. These memoirs run to 100,000 words. But how to present them as a coherent work? Would anyone outside his immediate family be interested in sifting through the anecdotes?

He asked me to help him with this. To ghostwrite, maybe. The original idea was to focus on his time at the steel plant, when he encountered such corruption that a contract was put out on his life, and he had to worry about tons of rolled-up metal "accidentally" dropping on him. But after interviewing him at length, I decided that limiting the book to that one period of time was a disservice to the rest of his story. The tales of his childhood, in that flyspeck town on Lake Superior, were so fascinating, so rich in detail, that they simply could not be discarded. Also, Frank's memoirs are exactly that—memories. He isn't one to look for larger themes, or even second-guess his actions, beyond an occasional, "Oh, I shouldn't have done *that*." He was a failure analyst by trade, but that doesn't mean he's inclined to analyze his own failures. He will acknowledge mistakes, of course, and he readily and almost proudly admits that he's failed much more than he's succeeded. But what he sees as a personal account of random events that happened to him, I view as a story of 20th century America itself.

Franklin St. John is a legitimate rags-to-riches tale, a Horatio Alger story—the sort of character who isn't much seen outside of fiction. He's the American Dream made flesh, a popular myth come to life.

"You're that rarest of things," I told him. "Something people talk about all the time, but hardly ever encounter: A self-made millionaire."

He looked at me with his mouth slightly open, an expression he often makes—and has always made, as evidenced by the sole baby picture that exists of him—when he is deep in thought. "I never thought about it that way," he said.

And there was the problem in a nutshell: Frank did not have the requisite distance from his subject to understand how much in his biography was *literary*. This literary quality is what I wanted to bring out, but I couldn't effectively do that while pretending to be him, as the ghostwriter must.

So we decided that *I* would write the book, from my point of view, and I would do my best to be critical, objective. A good biography is an examination of a life, after all, not just a simple chronicle of events.

"Maybe it will be a best-seller," he said, and I could see the familiar fire in his eyes. As an engineer, Frank favors quantifiable results: 4.0 grade-point averages, net profits, free throw percentage, NCAA Women's Basketball Championship trophies, and so on. He tends to view success in these terms, too—much to the consternation of my wife, who as an artist is more about the shades of gray.

"Maybe," I said, hedging, "although, I mean, that's beyond my control." I try to temper his expectations. After all, the odds of a book like this one winding up on a best-seller list are as long as…well, as the son of a plowman from the Upper Peninsula making multiple millions in metallurgy. Once you've achieved that sort of success, you must feel like everything else you try will succeed just as spectacularly.

And who am I to tell him otherwise?

PART ONE

MICHIGAN

Louis and Doris St. John in the front door—the only entrance—to the
St. John home in L'Anse, ca. 1952. The little girl is Franklin's niece,
Doris; in the shadows is his sister LaVerne.

1

WHERE HAVE YOU GONE, EXEPHIS GUINDON?

THE NORTHERNMOST EXTREMITY of the Upper Peninsula of Michigan is Keweenaw Peninsula, which extends like a dorsal fin into the chilly expanse of Lake Superior. In the armpit of that fin, nestled deep in the cove of Keweenaw Bay, is the town of L'Anse. The word is French for *cove*. Here, some two thousand people make their home, down from 2,500 in 1938, when Franklin Muriel St. John was born there, in a two-bedroom house with no indoor toilet.

L'Anse is lovely, especially in the summer, but it's cold and very, very remote: three hours from Green Bay, four hours from Milwaukee, six hours from Minneapolis, seven hours from Chicago, eight hours from Detroit. We hear so much about coastal elites and about Middle America, the so-called Heartland; Florida is Florida; Texas is Texas; and the Southern border has long been a political talking point. But the extreme north, in the middle of the United States, does not factor into the national discussion at all. It is Siberia. Few places in the country are as far away from the seats of power as Frank's hometown—geographically and culturally.

The Gaudrault family emigrated to L'Anse from Gentilly, Quebec, soon after the Civil War. They had colorful names: Thelesphore Gaudrault was the son of Joseph Gaudrault and the former Scholastique Baril. As the 19th century gave way to the 20th, the clan's very French surname was inevitably Americanized, or perhaps dumbed down, to Goodreau. Both of Franklin's grandmothers were descended from the Goodreau line, and were probably distant cousins. Both lived in L'Anse before their eventual husbands.

Dora Elizabeth Goodreau was the only child of Ephraim "Fram" Goodreau and Olive Alee. She was born in 1891, when her mother was already well into her thirties—ancient, for that time. Dora's husband was called Henri Rochan in his native Ontario, but Henry Rochon when he arrived in L'Anse on a sled one snowy day in 1907. One imagines him as Yukon Cornelius from *Rudolph the Red-Nosed Reindeer*, trudging through the ice and snow in search of something better. He found what he was looking for in Dora, who was just 16 at the time—17 years his junior.

"Could you imagine," Frank told me, "having some strange man in his thirties hanging around your house, trying to get with your 16-year-old daughter?" He shook his head. "But that was a different time."

Indeed, this was roughly the same year when Tevye, in *Fiddler in the Roof*, promises his daughter Tzaitel to his coeval, Lazar Wolf. One hopes that Dora liked her woodsman suitor more than Tzaitel liked hers. But whatever her true feelings, she bore Henry Rochon five children. The fourth of these, born on February 24, 1912, was Doris Eleanor Rochon—Franklin's mother.

Clarinda St. Germain was born to Georgianna Goodreau on July 26, 1881. Clara, as she was called, was married at 19 to the wonderfully-named Exephis Guindon, with whom she had two daughters. And then, one night, Exephis Guindon up and left, leaving no forwarding address: Here today, gone tomorrow. And even now, in the age of Google and Ancestry. com and 23 & Me, there is no trace of the guy. What leads a man to abruptly abandon his family I cannot say. Perhaps his departure was not a surprise. It may even have been welcome. Frank told me that his grandmother was something of a Runaround Sue, and that her infidelity might have led Exephis to bail. In the event, a few years into the new century, Clara suddenly found herself a single mother with two small children. But she was young and pretty and "wild," as Franklin put it, and so she seemed to have no trouble finding a second husband—and trading up.

The seventh of ten children, Simeon "Sam" St. Jean-Coitu came from a family of farmers in a village in northern Quebec. Farming bored him. He preferred adventure to agriculture. So he hopped a southbound train, in search of a better life. Sam couldn't speak a word of English. But he was charming, funny, warm—something of a merry prankster. "He always had a smile on his face," Franklin told me. "He was always laughing. But he was 100 percent a scoundrel. Oh, was he bad. And yet everybody liked him."

One of the people who liked him especially was the aforementioned Clara St. Germain. She may have been a single mother of two girls, but she was still in her mid-twenties, and, whether "wild" or not, clearly desirable. Here was a fetching woman with a house and two small kids—a ready-made family. Sam moved in, replacing the departed Exephis Guindon, ditched the "Coitu," and changed the spelling of his name to the more American "St. John." He took a job as a lumberjack.

The word *lumberjack* has a mostly benign connotation—red flannel, Monty Python, enormous breakfast platters—but Sam's day-to-day was no picnic. One wonders if he'd have been happier on his family's Canadian farm. As Frank writes in his memoirs:

> Throughout the long winter in the Upper Peninsula of Michigan, the lumberjacks lived in camps, which were actually shacks, and each shack had from 12 to 16 men. These

men would get up at about three in the morning and then make their way to the dining hall. There they were served a huge breakfast of bacon, eggs, bacon grease, pancakes, maple syrup, many bread products, pies, jam, butter, coffee, tea, milk, and probably some things I forgot. After breakfast, the men were transported by horse-drawn wagons, or by walking, depending on the distance to the work site. While it was still dark, the men began to cut and trim the trees. It is easy for me to simply state that the men cut and trimmed the trees, but I know that the work was extremely hard due the extreme cold as well as that all of the work was done by hand. There were no power tools as there are today.

The men worked until about six in the evening with a lunch break at midday in the woods. After completing their day's toil, they would make their way back to the camp for their final meal of the day. This routine was followed for six days with Sunday a day of rest. On Sunday, some of the men spent the day washing clothes and bathing. It didn't appear that the bathing part was very enticing. Remember that it was extremely cold in the woods of the UP. They accomplished the bathing by building a large fire to heat a large kettle of water and then did the best they could to clean themselves. I fully expect that it was not a priority in any sense of the word. When I was a boy in the 1940s, my father took me to a camp, and it was hard to realize how the men managed. The camp had a strong presence of body odor. I guess the men just got used to the conditions as they were.

Not only was Sam spending weeks at a time in these stinky camps, working every daylight hour in the freezing cold, but the work itself was dangerous. He was stocky and physically strong, but he was not invincible. In the winter, the logs were cut and stacked next to the frozen waterways. In the spring, the rivers thawed, and the logs were launched into the rushing water—carried downstream to a landing spot at the mouth of the river, where they were eventually transported to the saw-mills. This facet of the job was even more perilous than the initial felling of the trees. Logs would frequently jam in the river, and Sam would have to walk in, on top of the logs, and clear out the jam. Many a lumberjack broke a finger, a hand, an arm or leg performing this task. Others fell into the river and were crushed by the heavy logs. Sam was well aware of this risk, as this anecdote from Frank's memoir shows:

> During the loading of the lumber on one of the boats in L'Anse harbor, the men were fooling around on one of the platforms above the water and one of the men pushed Sam off the platform and into the water and Sam started yelling for help. The men on the platform thought that he was kidding, until one of the men realized that Sam wasn't kidding and that he was actually drowning. The men jumped into the water and pulled Sam to shore. After he was pulled to safety, one of the men said to Sam that he couldn't believe that he couldn't swim, because he had ridden the rivers for years. Sam's response was that, if you fell into the water, it didn't make any difference if you could swim or not, you would be killed by being crushed by the logs.

Despite his well-deserved reputation as a scoundrel, and his difficulty with the English language, Sam was respected among his colleagues for his arithmetical skills. The men were paid based on how many pieces they put on the lumber boats. They went to Sam to double-check the math on the wages they could expect. He was also a cutthroat cribbage player—savvy enough to add up the scores, and slippery enough to cheat, even when playing against his own grandson!

In 1905 the couple had a son—Louis St. John, Franklin's father; named for Sam's father—followed by four girls: Clarina, Molina, Georgiana, and Eva Henrietta, who was called Mary Ellen because, I guess, the other two names were not enough. Only when they were done producing children did the couple get married. Sam had trouble pronouncing his son's Americanized name, calling him "Loosh."

In Frank's recollection, his father's four younger sisters were all cold, and he did not much care for them. Mary Ellen/Eva once got in a bar fight, beating up some guy with her high-heeled shoe. Molina moved to Los Angeles, where she made a living as a sex worker of some kind. She was a homicide victim. I don't know any more details than that, and it seems like that was the family line, one everyone knew better than to delve into: *Aunt Molina was a prostitute who was murdered in a Hollywood hotel room.* In photographs, she is pretty and flapperishly fashionable, like a silent film star of that era—Norma Talmadge, say. There is a James Ellroy novel in there somewhere.

The two older half-sisters, Frank recalls fondly. Both of them managed to escape from the Upper Peninsula. One, Mary, wound up in Pontiac. The other half-sister, called Marissa, moved to Detroit, where she married. And it's to the Motor City that our story now turns.

2

LOOSH

To HEAR FRANK TELL IT, the St. John house of the early aughts was not a particularly happy one. Sam St. John was a "scoundrel." Clara St. Germain was "wild." Neither of them were strangers to drink. The two oldest girls left home as soon as they possibly could, with one of them opting for sex work in Hollywood rather than spending another frigid day in L'Anse. One imagines chaos, alcoholism, and, probably, abuse of some kind.

Here is an anecdote: One fine day, Louis "Loosh" St. John, Frank's father, walked from his house to visit his parents. (This was in the mid-1930s, so I'm skipping ahead in time for a moment.) As he came down the hill, he spied, through the front window, his mother performing fellatio upon a lumberjack, while his father slept drunkenly on the sofa a few feet away! He beat a hasty retreat and was gone before his mother noticed. That was when he was older, after he came back to town—as I said, I skipped ahead—but I doubt that Sam and Clara were any more careful when they were younger.

We know for certain that Louis was a victim of sexual abuse. At 11 or 12, he was molested by the town tailor. For the rest of his life, he was homophobic, in the strict sense of the word—terrified that because he had experienced not only arousal but orgasm at the hands of a man, he himself must be gay. As with many victims, he did not immediately tell anyone what happened. Maybe he was too ashamed. Maybe he didn't trust his parents to protect him. Instead, he skipped town—fleeing his own shame and humiliation. Just as his father, Sam, had hopped a train to *get* to L'Anse, so Louis hopped a train to escape.

At just 14 years of age, Loosh made his way to Detroit, the Motor City, where Henry Ford had established his base of operations. These were the boom years of the 1920s, and he was able to find work in a factory that dealt in automotive parts. He stayed with his half-sister and her family for the first year or two—until they left for the warmer climes and greener grasses of California.

Before I tell more about Louis in Detroit, let me pause here to marvel at how remarkable—how nuts, even—it is that I know the two intimate stories I've just related. The first one, concerning Clara and the lumberjack, was told to Franklin by his mother. The second, he managed to extract from his father later in life. The candor is refreshing. But we can safely assume that for every story we know about, there are hundreds of similar ones that we do not.

Louis St. John was, as they say, a *character*. He was charming, fun, and very funny. He cracked jokes almost constantly, and Frank claims never to have heard the same joke twice. Neither did Doris, apparently. "Mom told me that when they were first married, they would lie in bed and Louis would tell jokes, and she would laugh herself crazy," Frank writes in his memoir. Loosh had charisma, wiles, smarts, self-confidence, and above all, *presence*. It takes a special kind of person to leave home at 14, as he did—and to make a success of himself as a teenager. Even after his half-sister moved away, Louis remained in Detroit, eight hours away from home, working at the plant. By the time he was 22, he was a supervisor, boss to a crew of workers. He had a good job, a solid reputation, and his future prospects were rosy.

But that all came crashing down. Someone in the office stole some money from the warehouse. Because he was the manager, and had access to the loot, Louis was the prime suspect. His employers were so confidant in his guilt that they managed to have him locked in the county jail for over a month, awaiting trial (while in the hoosegow, he somehow contrived to have a liaison with the jailer's daughter—which sounds like the set-up for a dirty joke, although Frank insists it really happened). After a few weeks, the real culprits were discovered. Louis was released from jail, and his boss, abashed at what he'd done, offered to restore his job. Louis said no. ("He told him to have intercourse with himself," Franklin tells me, laughing.)

Fast-forward 10 years. Louis, now a plowman in L'Anse, married with three children, is asked to take the foreman job, overseeing the crew of plowmen. This was in the late 1930s. He was the logical choice: smart, experienced, well-liked. And it would have paid a lot more than what he made—no small consideration, for the breadwinner of a young family during the Great Depression. But he turned down the job. The head of a household that did not feature an indoor toilet—a man who went to the freezing-cold outhouse if he had to go #2 in the dead of winter—declined the promotion.

That was only the most recent of numerous opportunities Louis had shot down since returning from Detroit. At a Motor City speakeasy, he was offered a musical career by a talent scout who heard him sing; he declined. As an avid collector of scrap metal, Louis was approached in the 1930s by his friend Joe Dorsky, who proposed going in together on a scrap metal business; he said no. In 1942, the owner of a local tavern approached Louis, hoping he would buy the business; he turned the guy down. The musical career likely would not have worked out, the scrap metal business would have made him a small fortune during the war, and the tavern may not have succeeded, but it's not like Louis wasn't spending his free time and excess cash in a tavern regardless.

Franklin couldn't understand why Louis passed on so many opportunities, especially the promotion to foreman during the Depression. The notion that his father would walk away from such a blessing was unfathomable to Frank. He simply could not conceive of a reason why his old man opted instead to continue his life of drudgery. The answer: "After what happened in Detroit, I never wanted to be in charge of anyone ever again." Louis was so traumatized by being falsely accused of a crime—and put in the slammer for it!—that he was scarred for life. That one horrible experience informed every employment decision he ever made afterward. It also informed Frank's.

The father wanted to never be in charge again.

The son wanted the opposite.

AFTER HIS RELEASE FROM JAIL, Louis hooked up with a friend of his, an older fellow of some means, with a yen to see America. We don't know who this man was, how they met, or what the exact details of their relationship were, although Frank is under the impression that it was a paid gig. Louis spent a year in the company of this mystery benefactor, riding shotgun, as they drove hither and yon across the country. The goal was to visit all states in the Lower 48. Decades before the Interstate highway system, in one of those old-timey Fords found in black-and-white James Cagney films, the duo managed to hit 36 of them.

That Louis, who clearly had an appetite for adventure and little fear of the unknown, would want to take such a trip makes perfect sense—especially when he was young and brash. What better response to a month of incarceration than to get into a car, roll down the windows, and drive away as fast as possible? Even so, the lost year on the road is puzzling. It complicates the picture of Louis, who always struck me, in Frank's numerous stories about him, as a creature of habit, a pillar of sameness and stability. And the company of the mysterious older man, so soon after the abuse at the hands of the tailor, on what must have been an intimate sort of adventure—this was *not* among the usual tales Frank told about his father; it was one he remembered later—adds a wrinkle to the story. Was there something untoward about the road trip? Was Loosh, like his half-sister in L.A., dabbling in sex work? Or was it just two guys, one much older, determined to see the country? Again, we cannot know for sure.

In the event, soon after the end of the road trip, Louis went north to visit family in L'Anse. He was not planning on staying, but while he was in town, he went to a dance, where he met a 16-year-old girl by the name of Doris Rochon. The two of them hit it off—so much so that she got pregnant. Doris was reluctant to go "all the way" so quickly, but Louis was as cocky and confident as could be: "If you won't do it," he told her, "believe me, someone else will." She determined that this brash, handsome, cock-of-the-walk stranger was worth the risk, and gave her consent. The dance took place in 1928. The twosome would remain together until his death half a century later.

At first, Doris's father was not thrilled about the union. Henry Rochon was a widower—even though his wife Dora was much younger, she'd passed away when Doris was 14— and was so upset, he threatened to send her away to reform school, rather than allow her to marry the fun-loving father of her unborn child. Frank tells what happened next:

> My father was also so very angry at that threat that he decided that he was going to do something about it. With that in mind he went to Henry Rochon's house and barged into his bedroom, threw up the shade, and pinned him down in the bed and called him a "squaw-chasing son of a bitch," which he was. He told her father that Doris was not going to any reformatory; in fact, he was going to marry Doris.

I wonder, if Henry had been more eager to marry her off, whether Louis would have been as adamant about doing the right thing. As he usually did, Louis got his way, and he and Doris Rochon tied the knot. Within two years of that fateful dance, she gave birth to two baby girls: Loretta LaVerne and Doris Jeanette, both of them called by their middle names for some reason, born not quite a year apart. Also within two years of that dance, on October 29, 1929, the stock market collapsed, triggering a global depression.

After a few scary years, when the young family subsisted on rabbits and other wildlife, Louis found a job with the Michigan State Highway Department, on the road crew working a plow—he lucked into it in 1934—and managed to hold it during the lean years and, indeed, until his retirement in 1968.

The stock market may fluctuate, but in the Upper Peninsula, there is always snow.

THE BRASH, COCKY MAN who left home at 14, who road-tripped across the country before that was even a thing, remained in L'Anse for the rest of his life—living in the same house, drinking in the same bar, singing the same drunken bar songs, but never cracking the same joke twice.

The L'Anse house, located at 3 Greenwood Street, has taken on mythical proportions in the family lore. Frank was deeply ashamed of it at the time, and still speaks of it with disdain and sometimes terror, but the feelings associated with the place are not all negative. His childhood left much to be desired, as we will see, but even so, there were certainly good times, too.

The house itself was maybe 650 square feet, frugally and inefficiently heated by two poorly-placed wood stoves, its two small bedrooms separated by a tiny hallway in which was kept the chamber pot and, inconveniently, the crib where Frank slept until he was nine. There was a washtub in the kitchen, where the family took their biweekly baths. There was, famously, no indoor toilet. There was no hot water. There was no insulation. In the winter, Louis would pack snow around the house, as if it were an igloo, in a vain attempt to keep the heat in. He would collect wood from his plow job, and drive it home piled up through the convertible roof of his Model "A" Ford ("Oh, how I was ashamed of that car!" Frank told me). But no amount of wood could stave off the bitter Upper Peninsula cold. He recalls:

> In the winter it was unbearably cold in the house except if you stood right next to the stove. Warm clothing was absolutely necessary. At night the stove would go out and the temperature in the house would try to approach the outside temperature. On these cold nights, the one faucet we had in the house was allowed run, which keep it from freezing. At bedtime, Mother would take a clothes iron from the stove, pass it between the sheets, and we would jump in bed before the heat dissipated. Another trick was to use a hot water bottle to warm up the sheets before we jumped in bed and covered up our heads. The rugs that Mother had sewn out of rags for our floors were interesting. In the morning after a cold night the rugs would be curled up so that they looked like dead raccoons lying on the floor. They would stay in that position until my dad would start the fire in the morning, then as it got warmer in the house they would straighten out.

Whatever pittance was left over from his meager wages was spent taking Doris to the local bar. The St. John family *really* could have used the money from the promotion Louis turned down.

After two pregnancies not quite one year apart, Doris realized that most of what she knew about the birds and the bees had been misinformation. ("You may ask why they had two children so close together," Frank wrote. "Understand that Doris was only seventeen and knew little about birth control. Her mother-in-law told her that you couldn't get pregnant if you were nursing a baby. WRONG!!") She took charge of her body. To the consternation of her parish priest (more about *him* later, too), she began using birth control. She waited a few years before having a third child, a boy—but he died a few hours after delivery.

Two more years went by, and she gave birth to another son, called Louis Paul. She doted on the child, and was devastated when he died of fever at the age of two. A few more years went by, and on July 2, 1938, she delivered the last of her children, and the only one of her three sons to survive childhood: Franklin Muriel St. John. One might assume that he was named for the popular president, who was doing his best to lead the nation out of the Great Depression. In fact, Doris named him after her doctor, whom she was sweet on.

Doris was superstitious about her son, but also protective. She refused to have his picture taken, fearing that the camera was somehow to blame for the loss of Louis Paul. And she doted on the boy. His sisters were eight and nine years older than he, respectively, and they, too, kept close watch over him. The house might not have had a toilet, or hot water, but there was plenty of love and attention directed at young Frank. This was not limited to the terrestrial plane. He says that he felt, and still feels, the presence of his dead brother, Louis Paul, from the Other Side.

Frank wasn't quite the seventh son of a seventh son, yet there was something special, almost mythical, about the circumstances of his birth, in the living room of that small house. To his mother, he felt like the Chosen One.

And, in a way, he was.

3

BEASLEY'S

NOT ONLY WAS FRANKLIN THE BABY, but he was, as I mentioned, considerably younger than his sisters. As long as Laverne and Jeanette lived in the house, there was never a shortage of people to look after him. I've known my father-in-law for 23 years, heard more stories from him that I can recount, but I don't think he's ever once mentioned his early childhood, with one exception: a fond recollection of how an empty cardboard box and a wooden spoon kept him blissfully occupied for hours. His mother watched over him during the day, and at night, that responsibility fell to his sisters. So his first years on earth were spent in a cocoon of motherly and sisterly love and affection.

It was only after his sisters moved out that the stories begin. Both Laverne and Jeannie married young, so by the time he was nine years old, Frankie, as he was then called, found himself, for the first time in his young life, alone—often, to his horror, at night. It was *dark* on Greenwood Street when the sun went down, in that high Northern latitude, and nowhere as dark as his own home.

"I would walk into the house, alone," he recalls. "There was a cord that hung down from the ceiling light. I would move very slowly into the kitchen, waving my arm in front of me through the darkness, until I caught hold of the cord, and turned the light on. And even then, the light was dim. There were shadows everywhere. I developed a great fear of the dark."

The reason he would be alone at night is because his parents would spend almost every evening at Beasley's bar, on North Front Street, a short walk from the shores of Lake Superior. After dinner, Louis and Doris would pack their boy into their Model-A Ford—outmoded even then—and make the five-minute drive to the establishment. Young Frankie was not allowed inside. He would fidget by himself in the car, bored out of his mind, waiting for his parents to drink their fill. If they took too long, or he grew too bored, he would walk the mile back home—to the dark, empty, scary house. His nightly choices were boredom and terror.

Though young, Frankie was old enough to understand the economics of all of this. Money was tight. The house, famously, had no toilet. The old Ford was a source of much embarrassment. And yet when it came to entertainment—to drink—no expense was spared. Childhood boredom and terror evolved into adolescent resentment and anger. I don't know if Louis and Doris really went out every single night, or if it just felt that way in Frank's memory. But it doesn't really matter. He was the victim of parental neglect, and it traumatized him. He felt scared, abandoned, alone, unsafe. Seventy-five years later, he still has not forgiven his mother and father for this abdication of their essential duty.

But he doesn't blame his parents—not exactly. He blames their neglect on alcohol, a substance he abhors. Frank is not a teetotaler. He will have the occasional beer at dinner, if my wife and I are having one. But he has never been a drinker. A man of extremes, he operates under the assumption that a thirst for alcohol leads ineluctably to ruin—or, at least, to leaving one's young child alone in the car while one imbibes and carouses at the local saloon. So he took great care never to be thirsty. Franklin was a *work*aholic, not an alcoholic—and, ironically, often as absent for his own kids as his folks were for him, as we shall see.

He describes his parents as alcoholics, but I can't tell if they were addicted to alcohol, or just craved the company that the bar provided. Louis, especially, was an extremely extroverted person, with a love of adventure. It's hard to know what was more important: the booze or the camaraderie. The fact that he quit drinking, cold turkey, in his mid-fifties suggests it was the latter.

Franklin speaks of the establishment contemptuously, but to me, a night at Beasley's sounds like a good time. L'Anse is too cold for much of the year for outdoor gatherings, and most people lived in small houses like the St. John place on Greenwood Street, so the neighborhood bar was, in a sense, like a communal living room, where all the entertaining took place. Louis and Doris would down their beers, and there would be joking and laughing, dancing and singing.

"My father had a wonderful singing voice," Franklin told me, "but he would only sing at the bar."

"Only the bar? Not at work, or around the house?"

"*Only* at the bar."

The family owned a radio, but did not have a TV until long after Frank moved out, and their house was minuscule. They weren't readers. What else were they supposed to do all night? Their social life was clearly a priority to them, and especially to Louis—who had other reasons for wanting to frequent Beasley's. He was, Frank tells me, having an affair with Mena Beasley, the bar's comely proprietor.

Here is a story Doris told her son many years later, long after Louis died. It took place on a summer night in L'Anse, while Franklin was away at college. A touring musician, a pretty chanteuse, played a show at Beasley's, much to the delight of the St. Johns. After closing the bar, the three of them—Louis, Doris, and the nameless singer—wound up back on Greenwood Street, all three of them gloriously shit-faced, lounging on the double bed. Eventually Doris felt a headache coming on, and excused herself to lay on the couch, where she promptly passed out.

"But Mama," Frank said, his eyes wide, "don't you realize what they must have done when you left?"

She looked as if she had never once considered this. Then she laughed, and gave him a little wave. "Oh, what does it matter? I'm just glad he had some fun."

What did Louis tell her that night at the dance, when they first met? *If you won't do it, believe me, someone else will.* That established their dynamic and set the tone for their entire marriage. From that moment until his death in 1979, Doris was conciliatory to his desires. She lived her life trying to pacify him, to placate him, to satisfy his needs. If that meant going to Beasley's every night, so be it. If it meant leaving Frankie in the car, so be it. If it meant sleeping on the couch to facilitate an infidelity, so be it. She made the marriage work, mostly by subsuming her own hopes, dreams, and desires.

At the end of her life, Doris confessed to Franklin that she was never happier than in her final years, in the new house he built for her, liberated from the tyrannical whims of her late husband.

She, too, found the house dark and cold.

4

THE BOY WHO LIVED

IF FRANKLIN'S BIRTH SEEMED MIRACULOUS, as if destined to happen, so too did his childhood. He is the real-life Boy Who Lived. On three separate occasions, young Frankie found himself in near-death situations. On all three occasions, his life was saved—his guardian angel, hard at work.

The first near-miss was when he was 18 months old. He was eating an apple slice, and in his eagerness to consume the delicious fruit, he swallowed the whole thing. Doris had her back turned, only turning around when she heard a strange noise from across the kitchen. It was her greatest fear realized—her little boy was turning blue! She picked him up, brought him outside, turned him upside-down, and pounded on his back. The apple piece came flying out, and Frank began to cry—and, crucially, to breathe.

The second near-miss was when he was three. The St. John family joined a group of other families on a trout fishing expedition to a nearby river. Louis explained to Frankie that he should stay away from the riverbank, as there were sections that were not safe. He then, characteristically, ignored his son, focusing on his own fun. Frank recounts what happened in his memoirs:

> I actually recalled this incident in therapy many years later. I ventured out to see if I could see the fish and no one paid any attention to me and sure enough I fell through a hole

in the bank and was floating under water, when Mrs. Dault, pronounced *doe*, saw me in the water floating and pulled me up by the hair. I can still remember floating under water and I still have the deep fear of drowning. What else happened after I was pulled out of the water, I do not recall except I remember being wrapped in a blanket. I believe that this incident is directly related to my fear of water.

The third and scariest incident happened about a year after he almost drowned. It was a Monday, the day most French Canadian families do the washing. Doris had a wringer washer, and all the clothes were hung on the line to dry. On this particular day, it was raining, so she hung the laundered garments in the house to dry. Frankie, bored, was outfitted in his rubber raincoat and rain boots and sent outside to play. He wandered across the street, to the large empty field where neighborhood kids congregated. On this day, because of the downpour, the field was deserted. Running through the mudpuddles, Frankie found himself stuck in a sinkhole. The more he struggled to free himself, the deeper he sank. He screamed and screamed, terrified that the earth would swallow him up. Finally, one Mrs. Bishop, who lived in a house near the field, heard his cries and came to his rescue. She managed to pull him out, but his boots were never seen again. Later, he was told that it wasn't a mudpuddle at all, but quicksand!

Little Frankie did not much care for school, and was not much of a student—not at first. He loved his kindergarten teacher, but after her, he tells me, his elementary school teachers used to hit him.

"Why? What did you do?"

"Oh, I just wouldn't pay attention. I'd just get up and start wandering around—that sort of thing."

This is easy for me to imagine. My wife and I used to go to dinner with Frank at a restaurant called The Rustic Oak, which had a great salad bar. When we would get there the hostess would show us to our table, but he'd ignore her—he'd head straight for the salad bar for a bowl of soup. If he was like that as a septuagenarian, I can only imagine how restless he must have been at eight or nine.

When he was not in school or asleep, young Frankie was outdoors, occupying himself with the usual pastimes: sports, especially baseball, which he still loves; swimming (carefully!) in the creeks and in the freezing cold Lake Superior; playing cribbage and other card games with his father and grandfather; fishing; accompanying his father to work (he enjoyed this, because the Highway Department had running water, and he could take a hot shower there); sledding. He writes that his childhood memories involve "sports, fighting, and snow activities." From what I can gather, he was cocky, scrappy, and a bit of a loner.

As teenagers, Frankie's sisters were constantly at one another's throats. Their cramped living conditions didn't help. There was no privacy. They had to share a double bed, and their spoiled little brother was in a crib right outside. By the time she was 16, LaVerne had given up on school. She began to play hooky; Jeanie knew this but didn't rat her out, in spite of the bad blood between them. It could be useful, she thought, to have something on her sister, to use for leverage later on. Eventually, Louis discovered LaVerne's truancy, and punished her ("physically," Frank writes, and I shudder to imagine what exactly that means). The incident was so traumatic that LaVerne immediately ran off, fleeing to Marquette, 70 miles away, to be closer to her boyfriend, Loy "Sonny" Ellis. She never returned to the house on Greenwood Road. As soon as she turned 18, she and Sonny got hitched; the marriage lasted for 52 years, until her death in 2000.

With LaVerne out of the picture, Frankie graduated from the crib to the double bed, which he shared with Jeanie until she left home at age 18. "This is not a recommended thing," Frank writes, "but that was the only option open at the time. At nine years of age, I should have had a bed of my own and not be forced to share one with my sister. We did not have another room for me."

But it could have been worse. Frank was extremely close with Jeanie, who was definitely his favorite person from his childhood, and probably his favorite person period. He genuinely adored her, and she took good care of him on the many nights his parents were at the tavern. Sometimes she would take him with her on dates. On one of these, Jeanie's beau gave Frankie a quarter to "run around the block." He insists a quarter was a lot of money in those days. Years later, that young man, Roger LeBeau, was killed in Korea.

Because their daughters were only a year and six days apart, Louis and Doris decided to start LaVerne a year later in school, so the two girls would be in the same class. The plan almost immediately came to naught, as Jeanie was held back in first grade. Frank believes that if LaVerne had started on time, and if Jeanie had not been held back, his sisters may have graduated from high school. As it was, they both dropped out after tenth grade.

On the day she turned 18—October 11, 1948, an unhappy date for Frankie—Jeanette left home, following her boyfriend, Kenneth Uren, to Milwaukee. He recalls the sadness he felt, seeing her off at the train station. Not only would he miss his best friend, but he would also be left all by himself when his parents were at Beasley's. He was ten and a half, still young. Now it was just him and his parents.

"Uren" is pronounced "you-RENN," but to the wisecracking Louis, his new son-in-law was Kenny Urine, or, sometimes, Kenny Piss. Jeanie was not keen on trading in the stately "St.

John" for such a piss-poor surname, so she convinced him to swap out the U for a W, and they became Mr. & Mrs. Kenneth Wren. For the rest of his life, Frank visited his sister and her family (they had three kids: Dorene, Michael, Debbie) as often as he could.

"Oh, he loved visiting Aunt Jeanie," my wife told me. "He would just show up and plop himself on the couch, and she would wait on him, hand and foot. He loved it! She took good care of him. And he took care of her. He was always looking out for her, sending her money."

I met Jeanie's husband Kenny once—on a trip East, Frank brought him to our house to meet our young son, Dominick, who, like Kenny, was born on Christmas Day. He was a kind man, tall, with piercing eyes and a wonderful head of white hair.

5

ALTAR BOYS

THERE WERE TWO HILLS in L'Anse, and they formed a boundary between the Catholic side of town and the Protestant side. It wasn't exactly the Hundred Years War, but there was no love lost between the two factions—not much mixing, Frank recalls, between the two sides. Even though they went to the same school, Catholics and Protestants stuck to their own group.

A French-Canadian family with a saintly surname was obviously Catholic. But the St. John family had a strained relationship with the local church. After Franklin arrived, their third child raised during the Great Depression, Louis and Doris began to use birth control, as discussed. Money was already in short supply, the small house was crowded, and the last thing they wanted was another mouth to feed. At confession, Doris told the priest what they were up to, and the priest told her that, if her husband insisted on birth control, she should deny him sex. That didn't go over too well, as you can imagine. Once he realized why his wife was cutting him off, Louis went to the rectory, burst into the priest's office, grabbed him by the collar, and shoved him against the wall. "How dare you tell my wife what to do!" he shouted, among other choice words. Then, his anger sated, he stormed out.

During the homily the following week, the priest went into a tirade about birth control, inveighing against the very concept of family planning. How dare mortals try to play God, and so on—the usual bullshit harangue. He then told of the wayward husband who had dared to accost him in his chambers. Louis sat there, seething. Doris implored him to keep quiet. If he reacted, she correctly reasoned, everyone in the church would know it was them the priest was talking about. Somehow he managed to temper his anger and not give himself away. But it would be years before he returned to the church.

Frankie, however, continued to attend Mass. The Church was an important part of Frank's life growing up. He saw himself as a good Catholic boy, and prided himself on converting one of his friends:

> My friend Richard Ellis, or Dickie as he was called, did not go to any church, so I started taking him to church, and he actually became a Catholic. According to the Catholic Church, there is a reward in heaven for those who convert someone into the religion. Yeah!! There was an article written in the *Sunday Visitor* about the Conversion of Richard Ellis. The *Sunday Visitor* was a Catholic newspaper for the Diocese of Marquette.

In the twenty-twenties, we know that sexual abuse was rampant in the ranks of the clergy, but in the forties and fifties, priests were regarded as men of God, benevolent, blameless, virtuous, trustworthy. This was demonstrably untrue in L'Anse. Franklin tells story after story of priest after priest who put the moves on a friend, a cousin, a neighbor. There were so many incidents of abuse that it seems to me, with the benefit of hindsight, that this remote outpost in the Upper Peninsula was where the Church consigned predatory priests who were known abusers. As punishment, they were relocated from New York or California or Florida—from choice parishes—to the Siberia of northern Michigan. Thus the boys of Baraga County paid for the sins of their better-located coevals.[1] Like all good Catholic lads, Frankie served as an altar boy. And this succession of predatory priests was who Frankie and his friends and family served.

Frank had a cousin named Delmar Goodreau, of the family line that had lived in L'Anse for generations. At a family reunion, years after the event in question took place, Delmar shared his recollection of a confrontation between Frank and the parish priest. This discussion happened over dinner, at a banquet table.

"Remember the time you stood up to the priest?"

Frank did not remember the time he stood up to the priest.

"Yeah, he was making a move on you, and you swatted him away, and you pushed him up against the wall and told him to keep his fucking hands off you!"

As the eyes of everyone at the table turned to him, Frank smiled uneasily. It was clear that Delmar had a very clear recollection of this incident; he related the story with equal parts pride and awe. But Frank felt weird about taking a bow, because *he could not remember* this ever taking place. Either 1) he blocked it out, or 2) it never happened. Fighting back against a priest who was trying to molest you seems like the sort of thing one would remember. And Frank St. John had, and has, excellent recall. So why couldn't he access that memory?

Sexual abuse is one of Frank's lifelong fascinations. ("*Fascinations* is not the right word," my wife corrects me. "It's more like it haunts him. He's *haunted* by sexual abuse.") He has always been interested in psychotherapy, Freud, and trauma. He's seen *Spotlight*, the 2015 film about the *Boston Globe*'s reporting on the Catholic sex abuse scandal, at least two dozen

---

[1] Frank insists that this isn't true, that the bad priests of Michigan all came from the state, but were moved around the diocese, so they didn't stay in any one parish for too long. Either way, the point holds: the Church knowingly moved sexual predators to L'Anse.

times. Sexual abuse is a frequent topic of his conversation, one he will bring up, and return to, over and over again, the way other men might bring up baseball or politics. He was in therapy for years, and even claims to have memories of his past life—but no recollection of the altercation with the pedophile priest.

Memory is famously unreliable, especially memory of trauma. Given the reputation of the priests in L'Anse, and the stories of other altar boys being molested by them, it seems unlikely that a pedophile priest would not try to initiate young Frankie into his sick perversion. Frank may have been physically strong, smart, and possessed of high self-regard, but he was still a child. We would all like to believe we would react to a priest attempting to molest us the way Delmar claimed that Frankie did. Precious few actually do.

It's more like it haunts him. He's haunted by sexual abuse.

If I had to guess, I'd say that something unspeakable happened to Frankie and Delmar, something both of them were deeply ashamed of, in the private chambers of that sicko priest; to survive, Delmar invented the hero story, casting his cousin as the savior in his own personal revisionist history, while Frankie refused to allow his mind to ever remember it again.

6

SIRENS' SONG

WHATEVER MIGHT HAVE HAPPENED WITH THE PRIEST, Franklin's romantic life was unaffected. At all. All through high school and college, he was something of a lothario—clearly the son of the cocky ladiesman Louis, and the grandson of the "wild" Clara. In the 23 years I've known him, I've heard countless tales of his libidinous exploits. When I interviewed him for this project, he would recount some steamy story, and then coyly ask, "Greggie, are you going to put that in the book?" I could never tell if he asked because he didn't want me to, or to make sure that I did.

Before we get any further, let me assure the reader that no, I'm not putting these stories in the book. If he wants them out in the ether, he is more than capable of writing letters to *Penthouse Forum*, or whatever the equivalent is nowadays. However, ignoring all bedroom activity out of some antiquated notion of propriety means omitting a key facet of Frank's life. Also: the fact that I (and my wife, and my brother-in-law) know so much about this topic is also, in and of itself, revealing.

Here is what I *will* tell you: Processing all the stories of his glory days, themes begin to emerge.

First and foremost, Frank had enormous carnal appetites, and he placed great priority on their satiety. From a young age, he was very good at getting his needs met. Whether it was getting his mother to cook for him, or his sister to take him with her on her dates, he had a knack for getting women to give him what he wanted. This skill translated easily to his romantic life. As studious as he was, especially in college, there was *always* a girl. And if there wasn't, he would not be shy about finding one. He was like one of those birds in a *National Geographic* documentary that fly great distances for one little taste of nectar.

Second, he's a one-woman man. If Frank is with someone, he's with her. While his Catholic upbringing certainly informs this commitment to fidelity, I think his monogamous streak has more to do with efficiency than Christian morals. If a willing partner already exists, why waste time looking for alternatives?

Third, like many men who came of age in the fifties, Frank applies a double standard to his romantic conquests. From the sound of it, he had a field day during his high school and college years. If he met a woman with the same level of sexual experience, however—someone like "wild" Clara—he would quickly sour on her.

And, finally, while he was not afraid of commitment, per se, he did not apply the same standards to his girlfriends that he did to his future wives. He would date—and sleep with—women he liked, but when the prospect of marriage was raised, he ran for the hills. He seemed to have a sense that he was a catch, an ideal husband, and he wasn't going to get pinned down by just anyone. There are more than a few stories of his various girlfriends spinning lies about him being the father of an unborn child, to try and trick him to the altar. It calls to mind Odysseus, strapped to the mast to resist the urge of the sirens' song—although Frank did not keep himself tethered to a mast.

I bring this up now, at the end of the Michigan section of the book, because it relates to what everyone in the family knows as The Airplane Story. But before we get to that, let's quickly cover the rest of Frank's time in his home state:

He was a good if not superlative student in high school, but his grades and his test scores were solid enough to attract the interest of Michigan Tech, the state's technological university, in Houghton, forty minutes away. A L'Anse neighbor was a metallurgical engineer, and seemed to have steady job prospects; Frank excelled in math and science, so he decided to go into that rather specific field. He took a series of tests in the hope of obtaining a prestigious national scholarship, but, as he wryly recalls, "The results of the tests were that I didn't get the prize." He did, however, win the State of Michigan scholarship, which, while not as coveted, did cover his tuition for four years of study.

After a short stint working at a butcher shop, Frank decided he couldn't work and study at the same time, so he left the dorm and began to commute to school, 35 miles away, with a group of five other students from Baraga County. All six of them would pile in the car every day and make the trek to the campus—even when it snowed! This passage from his memoirs calls to mind the lament of the grandparent who claims he walked seven miles to school:

> There were six of us, and I only had to drive every sixth day. By the way, classes were held six days a week. Cars in the 1950s did not have a center console, so three people could sit in the front seat. Also, there were no seat belts in the cars to take up additional room. There is another point: The average snow fall for my four years of college was over 200 inches a year. In fact, my junior year the snow fall was almost 250 inches. In my four years in school we never missed a day of school, because of snow or anything else for that matter (except for one term in my sophomore year, where I put romance ahead of everything else). There was one incident that I remember. There was a 20-plus inch storm, and we got stuck about 10 miles from school. Five of us got out of

the car and took shovels out of the trunk and shoveled and pushed the car through the snowbanks, and we made it to school basically on time.

All through the first few years of college, Frank had an on-again-off-again relationship with his high school sweetheart. Her real name is very cool, so much so that I borrowed her surname to give a character in one of my novels. But for our purposes, let's call her Anna. As I said, Frank and Anna were on-again, off-again for years. And there were lots of fireworks with her parents, who were Lutheran, and couldn't stand him. At one point, they sent Anna to California so she wouldn't date him anymore.

But his junior year, she came back to L'Anse to visit, and they were very much on-again—even though, unlike with his other girlfriends, the two of them never went "all the way." Instead, she did to him what his "wild" grandmother Clara did to the lumberjack. I hesitate to even mention this, but it's relevant to the story.

Junior year of college, Frank is chosen to interview for a prestigious summer internship in Chicago. They fly him there, to meet with him face to face. It's a big deal. On the flight home from O'Hare, he's sitting next to a fellow about his age, maybe a few years older. Frank strikes up a conversation with the guy. The guy asks where he's from. "L'Anse." "Oh, really? Do you know a girl named ___?" Frank recognizes the name, of course, because it's his on-again girlfriend. But he doesn't say so. He wants to see where this is going. "I've heard the name," he says. "But she was ahead of me in school."

And now it gets interesting. The guy—let's call him Jack Brody—proceeds to tell Frank about Anna, how he works with her in the medical center, and how she gets around with all the men there, how she just loves to...well, you get the idea. Brody *is* one to kiss and tell—even some stranger sitting next to him on a plane. And Frank just listens, and nods, and never reveals that the woman Brody is slut-shaming is the current love of his life.

The next time he sees Anna, he acts like everything's jake. They go to dinner. They go dancing. They dance slow and close, and he gets her revved up. Out in the parking lot, they get into the car, and she's ready for business. Frank stops her. "Do you know a fellow named Jack Brody?" And her face goes white. "How did you…"

That was the end of the relationship. Soon after that humiliation, Anna and her parents all left for California. Frank didn't see her again until their 25th-year high school reunion. She shot daggers at him the whole time.[1]

And while he stayed another year to finish his schooling, it was the end of his time in Michigan.

The Airplane Story is important because it changed the entire trajectory of his life. Instead of marrying Anna, and probably staying somewhere close to L'Anse, he decided to break up with her, and of the three job offers that came upon graduation, he took the one in Connecticut—not because it paid the most money, but because it was the farthest away from his hometown.

---

[1] I've distilled the Airplane Story down quite a bit, for purposes of flow. The chronology is simplified, and I've omitted a few colorful details, such as: 1) Anna's parents falsely accusing Frank of trying to marry her so she didn't go back to California; 2) Frank confronting them; and, for good measure, 3) Loosh also confronting them, which freaked them out so much that they literally left town. There is some weird karma going on with Frank and Anna.

PART TWO

CONNECTICUT

Frank St. John at age 17.

7

ROCKIN' AND A-REELIN'

THE REGENTS HAD A HIT IN 1958, later made famous by the Beach Boys, that went like this:

Went to a dance,
Lookin' for romance
Saw Barbara Ann
And I thought I'd take a chance.

In 1960, Franklin St. John made the "Barbara Ann" song lyrics come true. He really did go to a dance (at the Polish Hall in Hartford, Connecticut). He really was looking for romance (although perhaps "romance" is a bit euphemistic for what he had in mind). He really did see a woman named Barbara Ann (last name of Powell). He really did take a chance—and things worked out so well, he wound up marrying her.

Connecticut was not the Upper Peninsula, and Barbara Powell was not like any of his Michigan paramours. Most of his former flames had never even been to Detroit. Barbara was born in the Bronx, grew up in Queens—in Astoria, not far from where my wife and I would one day have an apartment—and had a New York sophistication that Franklin had never encountered before. He was used to being cock of the walk, the center of attention. He was used to women coming on to him. He was used to being seen as a "good catch," as husband material, and running away as soon as the topic was broached. He was used to being openly, almost desperately, desired, by wide-eyed women who saw him as their ticket out of L'Anse. Barbara Powell acted like she didn't give a shit. She liked him fine, but she could take him or leave him. This was a new dynamic for Franklin, and he relished it.

Barbara Powell was his first true love.

She was born in the Bronx, as mentioned, to Estelle and Walter Powell—the third of four children, and the only girl. The last name suggests a stuffy, almost aristocratic family, which is probably why Walter chose it. After his release from prison for forging checks, he wanted something more blue-blood.

Walter's real last name was Wojewódzki; it is the same root word as *voivode*, a member of the Polish nobility. Technically, he was born in Russia, but only because Russia occupied Odessa at the time, and Poland proper did not exist after the Partition and before the end of the Great War. He was a lovable scoundrel, cut from the same cloth as Frank's grandfather, Sam, but infinitely more audacious—and handsome. In one old family photo, he is on a beach, shirtless, playing a ukulele for Estelle. Tall, blond, athletic, chest puffed like a peacock, he looks like he could play center field for the Yankees. But he was no outfielder. Walter was a swindler and a con artist, a tax cheat and a felon, a philanderer and an alcoholic, and a gifted (and probably self-taught) piano player—a musical talent passed down through the generations to my brother-in-law and my wife. His nominal occupation was traveling salesman, and he would spend the winter months in Florida hawking his wares, while his family stayed put in New York or, later, Connecticut.

Frank is convinced that Walter had a second family in the Sunshine State. I'm not sure if he came to this conclusion on his own, or if he picked it up from things Estelle or Barbara might have let slip. It sounds like something from a bad dime novel. Either way, it was not something openly discussed. But a few years ago, my wife confirmed Frank's wacky hypothesis! The genealogy site 23 & Me showed her with relatives named Powell in Florida—close enough to be first cousins. She started an exchange with one of them that went along pleasantly enough, but once she floated the idea of Walter and the second family, all communication ceased.

It's hard for me to wrap my mind around the sociopathy required to maintain two separate families, in two different states, each ignorant of the other. That's the sort of thing you read about in dime novels, as I said, or TV shows set in the nineteenth century. But Walter Powell was an actual, honest-to-God bigamist. My wife, who holds a master's degree in mental health counseling, agrees with my amateur assessment of Walter as suffering from narcissistic personality disorder. "He definitely had those qualities, from what I understand," she says. "And my mother *definitely* had traits of being raised by a narcissist."

You'd think the family he left in the winter cold each year would be resentful, but no; among the Powell children, the patriarch was regarded as a hero, a family man, almost a saint. Well into old age, they all rushed to his defense, sung his praises, spoke of him with something like awe. Again: he was a scoundrel. He was gone half the time, and when he did come home, he was usually drunk. No doubt he was a fun guy, a barrel of laughs, and tickled the ivories like a champ, but for all his charms, he was objectively not a good person. Nevertheless, his kids were in his thrall until their dying days.

Estelle, who must have at least *suspected* his infidelity, was less enthused with her wandering-eyed spouse. Walter essentially abandoned her for months on end, leaving her alone with four children, none of them particularly easy, and it's not like he was out prospecting gold or striking oil. Money was tight. She never knew when he'd be coming back. And when he did return, the entire family had to pretend he was an uncle; if the landlord knew she was married, and not the single mom she claimed to be, he'd have raised the rent. They all played along with this elaborate ruse, this long con—his own kids calling him Uncle Walter—but Estelle had her limits. She once stabbed him with a steak knife, which doesn't bespeak of marital bliss. The blade was dull, the story goes, so he calmly withdrew it, fixed up his wound, and went about his business. My guess is, it was not the first time someone had stabbed Walter Powell—probably with good reason!

If there was dysfunction, mental illness, substance abuse, and violence in the Powell household, there was also genius. The firstborn, also named Walter, came along in January of 1929. He attended Manhattan Aviation High School and served in the Air Force at the end of the Second World War. After his military service, he enrolled on the G.I. Bill at the University of Connecticut, completing both a B.A. and M.A. in history; later in his career, he got a J.D. from Western New England College Law School and a Ph.D. from the University of Sarasota. He taught political science for 44 years at Slippery Rock University, serving for a time as department chair. Outside of his academic and legal career, he was famous for his passion for military aviation, acquiring enough stuff to open a modest museum. So: not too shabby, for the oldest of four children from a more or less broken home.

Each succeeding child was more brilliant, but also more tormented by mental illness. Richard, the second son, was the writer of the family. He was big-hearted, warm—the uncle most concerned with keeping the family together—but his drinking problem torpedoed his ample promise. When I came into the family in 2000, he was living in Belize, which, for an American citizen at that time, was a "last resort" sort of move.

The baby of the Powell clan, whom everyone, Franklin included, agreed was the most brilliant, was also the most screwed up. Donald started drinking at age twelve or thirteen, and basically never stopped. (Franklin, who, as I mentioned, is not a drinker, would often cite Donald's immediate descent into alcoholism as a reason he shied away from imbibing.) He moved from one job to another until things fell apart, and unlike the other Powell kids, he never really left home; Estelle was always on hand to clean up his mess. He never married, couldn't hold a job or a relationship, was a depressive. He tried numerous times to kill himself, each attempt more outlandish, before finally succeeding at age fifty. His was a tragic life story.

In this chaos was Barbara—seven years younger than Richard, two years older than Donald. She was a decent piano player and a great singer. She'd inherited her father's charm, and both her parents' good looks. Her confidence in her attractiveness was so bountiful as to approach the delusional. At the end of her life, in a Connecticut nursing home, she still believed absolutely that she was the hottest woman in the building; I can only imagine what she must have been like at 22. And she was *funny*. She had a ribald sense of humor that would have been right at home at Beasley's bar in L'Anse, an establishment she probably would have enjoyed. The woman Frank met and fell in love with at that dance presented as gorgeous, confident, talented, wisecracking, smart, and a bit naughty—a woman with all her shit together.

But Barbara didn't have all her shit together. Beneath that confident exterior, she was wrestling with demons of her own. Frank liked this, too, up to a point. He liked to be the savior. He liked to play the part his cousin Delmar cast for him in the story about the priest—the fearless hero. In 1960, though, none of this was apparent, just as it wasn't in 1962, when they tied the knot. The first three or four years of their relationship were happy ones, best as I can tell. He had a decent enough job, as a metallurgical engineer at the Pratt & Whitney company, and a dish of a wife who happily consented to his lusty advances even when he came home unannounced for lunch.

Franklin didn't, and doesn't, approve of cigarette smoking, and Barbara was a smoker. He insisted that she quit before they got married, and she told him sure. But she didn't quit. She just snuck her smokes on the sly. A few months after the wedding, he came home and caught her lighting up at the kitchen table.

"Barbara," he said, "you promised me you'd quit!"

"What are you gonna do," she said, blowing smoke at him like Sharon Stone in *Basic Instinct*, "leave?"

In 1962, he had no desire to leave. He'd have to acquiesce to her bad habit. It was a small price to pay for having his basic needs met. It was only after Louis was born, in 1964, that Barbara's mental health took a turn for the worse. By then, Franklin had changed jobs, from the low-level gig at Pratt & Whitney to a more senior position as a failure analyst—in a department honeycombed with supposedly rehabilitated Nazis.

8

HEIL, HITLER'S ROCKET SCIENTISTS

OPERATION PAPERCLIP, the top secret federal program in which ex-Nazi scientists and engineers were covertly spirited to the United States after the war, was not declassified until 2012. Before then, there was no official explanation for why expatriated Germans turned up in American manufacturing plants in the late 40s/early 50s. But there they were.

When Franklin took a new job at Avco Lycoming in 1962, the senior management had an entire contingent of what appeared to Frank to be Nazis. Their leader, Herr Dr. Anselm Franz, wore a long leather jacket of the kind favored by the Gestapo. All that was missing was the Third Reich stripes—although you could still see the place where they had once been. No one at the company knew for sure if their colleagues had been Nazi party members two decades ago. If pressed, they almost certainly would have assumed that, no, there were not Hitler disciples running American gas turbine manufacturing facilities. But their obvious Germanness was a running joke.

"Maybe if the Nazis had won the war," quipped Franklin's friend Jim, a World War II veteran, "the Germans would be working for us instead of the other way around!"

Decades later, after learning about Operation Paperclip, Franklin became convinced that the Germans he worked with at Lycoming were, indeed, Nazis. The top scientist on the premises, Dr. Franz, certainly fit the profile. He worked for five years at Wright-Patterson Air Force Base, outside of Dayton, Ohio. The stipulations to come to America were five years of labor, a sort of indentured servitude, for the U.S. military; after that, they were free to do as they pleased, granted full citizenship, and any record of their involvement with Hitler expunged from the record.

In hindsight, this seems almost unthinkable. Why we would grant safe passage to Nazis? But at the time, there were compelling, if morally dubious, reasons. After Germany surrendered, the Allies occupied the Western part of the country. The Soviets wound up controlling East Germany for almost 50 years. They also wound up controlling anyone unlucky enough to live in that part of the country for that length of time. The German scientists were brilliant. They'd developed a revolutionary gas turbine engine, in part to combat the Allied bombing operations, but the invention was not ready until 1945—too late to be of much help. Even so, there was enormous intellectual property in Germany, housed in the brains of its top scientists. Rather than let these men, and their big-brained ideas, wind up in the hands of the Soviets, our clandestine services devised a way to secret them into the United States, so that we could benefit from their technological know-how. There's a show on Amazon Prime called *The Hunters* that dramatizes the meeting at which this decision took place—a bunch of older white men, oblivious to the moral perils of, essentially, pardoning war criminals.

Franklin worked in the gas turbine division at Lycoming—the same gas turbine engine developed by Nazi scientists during the war. Here are his recollections of the alleged Nazis who were his colleagues:

Some of the names of the men that worked under these conditions at Wright Patterson that I remember were as follows:

Dr. Anselm Franz headed the group. He also headed the operation in Germany during the war. As I remember from my limited contact with the man, he was mild-mannered and quite reserved. Next in command was Dr. Wolfgang Adenstadt. He was anything but mild-mannered. He was extremely intelligent, loud, and demanding. When I was employed at Lycoming, I worked under his direction. Next was Dr. Klein, who headed the Mechanical Engineering group. He was quiet and very nice to most everyone. He had what I called 10X eyeballs. When a failure of an engine arrived at Lycoming, Herr Dr. Klein would come to the Laboratory to examine the failure with me. I always had a 10X magnifying glass with me to examine the fracture surfaces in order to detect the presence of a fatigue failure. If there was evidence of a fatigue failure, it indicated that there was a design problem and not necessarily a material's problem. Dr. Klein would close one eye and use his other eye to examine the fracture surface, whereby I had to use my 10X magnifying glass in order to examine the fracture surface. Because of this I claimed that he had 10X eyeballs. By the way, I never said this to his face.

Also, there was Dr. Belitz, who was involved with engine design. If there was evidence of a fatigue failure, Dr. Belitz would be called in immediately. He then would have Mr. Klein come and confirm the need for an improvement in the design of that section of the engine. I'm not sure what Mr. Klein's job was, but he looked and acted like a Gestapo agent. Maybe he was the Gestapo representative at Lycoming. (This is a joke.)

In 1951, this cluster of almost-certainly-ex-Nazi scientists from Wright-Patterson acquired a huge manufacturing building in Stamford, Connecticut. During Korea, it was used by Chance-Vought for aircraft production. The executives obtained contracts from the Department of Defense to develop a gas turbine engine, an improved version of what they'd devised in Germany during WWII. But it wasn't *all* Nazis. A number of former Air Force officers who had been working with the German scientists in Dayton also joined the company. Two of these men, American ex-military officers, headed up the Materials Development Department at Lycoming. They were brought aboard by Herr Dr. Adenstadt—the loud, demanding one.

When he went for the interview at Lycoming, Frank was 24 years old. He'd been married for two months. The rebellious, anti-authoritative streak he'd repressed for most of college and his early working life was becoming harder to tamp down. He was cocky, brash. He managed to impress the heads of the R&D and the Failure Analysis departments, who brought him to meet the manager of the Materials Development Laboratory, an intimidating former Air Force engineer named Bill Freeman.

There were three chairs in a row, facing an empty desk. Frank took the middle chair, flanked by the two department heads. They sat. They waited. "It felt like waiting in the principal's office, waiting to be disciplined for some infraction," he later recalled—a situation in which he often found himself, in his school days. After waiting for a good five minutes, the three of them sitting in awkward silence, the door opened, and in walked a tall, thin, well-dressed and surprisingly young man, the *New York Times* tucked neatly under his arm. He put the paper on the desk, took a seat behind it, and said, in lieu of a proper introduction, "What's the composition of gamma prime?"

If the intent was to intimidate Franklin, it backfired. To the contrary, the situation pissed him off. "If I want to know the composition of gamma prime," he snarled, as the two department heads cowered in their seats, expecting the worst, "I'll look it up in a book. If you want to know my thoughts on failure analysis, well, here goes," and then he launched into the sort of smarty-pants monologue you might see in a movie. (While I'm sure he has embellished this story a bit in the last 60 years, Franklin *does* have the ability to riff when he wants to).

When he was finished, Freeman looked at the head of Failure Analysis and gestured to a side office, where the two of them repaired. Frank looked at the R&D head for assurance, but found none. But Freeman emerged a minute later, offering him the job on the spot.

A few months later, Frank was sitting at his desk, working on a report, when he sensed someone standing behind him. He looked up to find Freeman, peering over his shoulder.

"You know," he said, "when you started here, you were a real tiger."

"Still am, Bill," Frank shot back. "I still am."

So it was that my father-in-law, unbeknownst to him, began to work for the Germans. It was better pay and more responsibility than Pratt & Whitney, and more intellectually demanding. He befriended a clutch of his new colleagues, including Jim the World War II veteran, as he participated in the workplace social life, the softball games, the bowling leagues, the drunken office parties—and pissed off more than a few people, as we shall see.

I wasn't able to verify the subordinates, despite some of their wonderful, almost parodic names, but Anselm Franz was famous in his field. He was born in Austria in 1900 and died 94 years later. In 1944, he developed the Jumo 004, the world's first mass-produced turbojet engine—unfortunately for the Nazis, too late to preserve the Third Reich. When he emigrated to the U.S., as part of Operation Paperclip, he turned his attention to producing what other large companies were not. This is how he came to develop the T53, a turboshaft engine used for helicopters, which powered the Bell Aircraft UH-1 Huey and AH-1 Cobra choppers and the OV-1 Mohawk ground attack aircraft. None of this means anything to me, but I'm sure my wife's Uncle Walter, with his military aviation museum, would have approved.

That Franklin wound up spending his formative work years in the presence of ex-Nazis is ironic. Years later, in psychotherapy, he was able to recall so far back in the past that he had what he describes as a past-life memory. In it, he himself is a German soldier, before the invasion of Poland that started the war, but well after Hitler was in power (Frank was born in 1938, and so, if you believe in this sort of thing, his last life ended in 1938). He is a prison guard. When ordered by his Nazi superior to shoot one of the Jewish prisoners, he refuses, and so he is shot through the temple. This may be reincarnation, or his mind playing tricks on him, but the story is perfectly plausible. His friend Jim told him similar tales, of German soldiers too lazy to file paperwork on prisoners, who shoot them dead instead. Also, it is very much like Franklin to refuse a direct order on principle, especially at work.

In the event, Frank found himself working side by side with Germans, some of whom he now knows for sure were actual Nazis, in Connecticut of all places.

9

FAILURE ANALYSIS

IT'S DIFFICULT FOR AN ENGLISH MAJOR like me to picture what goes on in a factory that produces aircraft engines. I get frustrated building houses out of Legos. The heavy industry Franklin worked for in those days, to me, is akin to sorcery. Some of the more fascinating parts of his memoirs concern his work successes: some difficult problem would arrive on his desk, and he would somehow determine what exactly went wrong and fix it. He was a metallurgist, and a damned good one. Here is an excerpt that involves a key event in his life—when he met his future business partner, Walter Jensen:

> Mr. Freeman wanted to establish a foundry to cast experimental blades for the turbine section of the gas turbine engines. He gave me the responsibility for purchasing a vacuum melting furnace. I looked at three different manufacturers. One of the three offered me a $2000 bribe, if I chose his system. I did not choose his system, not because of his offer, but because one of the other systems was better in my opinion. I ended up buying an Inductotherm system. Now that we had a vacuum melting facility we needed some experienced technicians to make this area run smoothly.
>
> At this point an event took place that changed the direction of my professional career and my life in general. We needed someone who understood vacuum systems and

had experience in directional solidification. Enter Walter L. Jensen into my life. Walter came from a research facility of Pratt & Whitney, where he was working on directional solidification of nickel-base gas turbine blades. Directional solidification is a method of going from the liquid to solid state under controlled conditions, which gives better properties to the part being produced. Walter was assigned to be one of my technicians to help in our experimental foundry. I had never experienced a technician with so much innate skill and ability to get a task done. I liked him so much that I talked Dr. Berry into hiring Walter to help me in my American Foundrymen's Society research project on directional solidification. We worked evenings and on weekends. It was amazing to me how he structured our experiments to get the material to solidify from bottom to top. I won't go into the technical details, because I can't imagine anyone would care except for those directly involved in the project. Both of the areas where we were working on directional solidification brought Walter and me in close contact and we became more than just co-workers. We became friends.

"Directional solidification" sounds like something a comic book writer would make up—an obscure field of study that Lex Luthor was into that would help him cast synthetic kryptonite. Franklin even explains what the term means in that paragraph, but all of it is so foreign to me, it may as well be written in Attic Greek. Put it this way: if some Nazi-adjacent brainiac asked *me* about the composition of gamma prime, I would assume he was referencing the title of a sci-fi novel, or a piece of music. Frank was that rare creature in the world of metallurgy—which, like many sciences, comprises a lot of introverts who don't play well with others: smart enough to grasp the science, but also both confident and charming. This combination of skills would pay handsome dividends later in life, when he and his new BFF Walter Jensen kicked off their own business.

If you got on his bad side—and a lot of people did—the twentysomething Frank St. John could also be kind of a dick. Among his work colleagues, I'm sure there was no shortage of men who wanted to sock him in the jaw. Here's one example: Lycoming had a bowling team. Back in Michigan, Frank spent a lot of time at the lanes, so he was well acquainted with that particular subculture. A new hire showed up one day, something of a braggart, who boasted of his bowling prowess. In the local league, he'd maintained a 180 average—quite good, for a rec league. "Twenty bucks says you don't do it this season," Frank challenged him, in front of everyone. The poor sap accepted the bet. Halfway through the season, our would-be Earl Anthony had a 168 average—good, but not good enough. "Tell you what," Frank said. "I'll give you a chance to make your money back. Double or nothing, your average isn't this high at the end of the year." The guy took the bet, and once again, he lost. Frank was $40 richer, which in those days was not an insignificant pile of cash. He'd cut the braggart down to size, and for that, was probably seen as a hero among some of his workmates. But he'd also made an enemy, for no good reason. Not that the bowling champ would come back to bite him in the ass. Throughout his life, Frank had an uncanny ability to sense who he could attack and who he should be careful with.

He also took great care not to put himself in compromising positions. He kept his wits about him. In those days, the office social life revolved around drinking. At the annual Christmas party, Bill Freeman would order industrial grain alcohol, ostensibly for some metallurgical purpose. Instead, he'd use it to spike the punch. We used to do this in college—if you made a punch bowl out of your garbage pail, which you lined with a thick plastic garbage bag, you have to put the juice in first, because unadulterated grain alcohol will eat through the plastic bag. It's serious stuff. So the Christmas parties would see these scientists guzzling 180-proof fruit punch. On one occasion, a disgruntled employee lost his shit at his boss, and when Monday came, got a pink slip. On another, Frank, sober as a judge, walked in on one of the secretaries getting it on with a half-passed-out technician, while another dude was doing his best to convince her to switch partners. Frank reprimanded them, but none of them paid him any heed. (If any of them were able to remember the incident the next morning, they probably thought of him as some kind of narc).

Sometimes, Frank's maverick attitude worked to his disadvantage. One Friday afternoon, he was summoned to Bill Freeman's office.

"By Monday morning," the boss told him, "I need 200 SM200 blades on my desk, ready to ship."

These blades, cast in a nickel-based alloy, were being used in engines for a special military project. It was the highest priority to get the order done.

The two operators were George List, and Franklin's friend and eventual business partner, Walter Jensen. They received time-and-a-half for working Saturday and Sunday, and Frank reports "little complaining" about having to come in on short notice. As the failure analyst, Frank would not need to physically be at the plant, but had to be on call, in case anything went awry.

He was at a party with Barbara that Saturday night when George List phoned from the plant. The vacuum system had failed. That meant that Freeman might not get his 200 blades. Frank called up Walter, and the two of them met at the plant.

"See?" George said. "The little light isn't on."

Frank and Walter examined the system, expecting the problem to be enormous. It was not. As it turned out, the little light was wired in series with the system, rather than in parallel; that meant that if the bulb was blown, nothing else would be getting power. As soon as Walter replaced the light bulb, the thing worked like a charm. Everyone went back to work, and Bill Freeman had his 200 blades.

"Great job, Frank," Freeman told him that Monday. "You should take the rest of the day off."

And here is where the maverick attitude cost him. "No thanks," Frank shot back. "I have my regular work to do."

As it happens, there was no real urgency with the 200 blades. They sat in the inspection area for two weeks, and after that, it took a few more weeks for them to be machined. The whole thing had been a power play, Bill Freeman flexing his muscle for no good reason. It rankled Frank that he had to work for someone else—*anyone* else, but especially a power-hungry schmuck like that guy.

10

EXIT 18

Barbara Powell's uncle, Stanley Segay, was what was termed in those days "mad." He thought he was a prophet. He heard voices. He had long conversations with birds. He lived the end of his days in what was termed in those days an insane asylum.

My wife has a master's in mental health counseling, and is well versed on the various DSM classifications of mental illness. She is also Barbara's daughter, and knew her as well as anyone. And even she doesn't know what her mother's formal diagnosis should have been. *Schizophrenia* is a blanket term that, as I understand it, is used only when more specific diagnoses aren't applicable. When she was on her meds, Barbara could function. When she was off her meds, she broke with reality, she sat at the kitchen table, drinking coffee and smoking cigarettes, writing page after page in her notebooks. I've seen the notebooks. Nothing she wrote made any sense at all.

Frank knew how to handle the Nazis at Lycoming, and his pompous, hard-ass boss, and he knew which of his colleagues to befriend, which to ignore, and which to call out for their false bravado—as with the bowling guy. But he was ill-equipped to handle his wife. He loved her dearly. He was passionately attracted to her, and they had a good and active sex life (that we all know this is a point of great irritation to my wife and my brother-in-law). But she was difficult for him to get along with. Whatever innate skills he possessed in dealing with people simply did not apply to Barbara.

The first years of their marriage seemed to go fine. However, Frank wasn't home much. He worked long hours, and when he wasn't at his primary job, he was doing side gigs, or in night school. My sense is that he'd wake up, go to work, occasionally come home for lunch and a quickie, go back to work, come home for dinner, go to night school, come home, have sex again, and crash. "She was a very sexual lady when she was young," he told me. As I see it, there didn't seem to be the requisite time or space for a deeper relationship to develop.

On the weekends, he also worked, and the schedule was more of the same. Barbara had a small circle of friends, but she spent an inordinate amount of time home, by herself. She played the piano, and she sang, and she played with the cat, and she shopped, and she planned out meals to cook. But she must have been bored out of her mind.

On September 9, 1964, Louis Neal St. John was born. He was named after Franklin's father; god knows why Barbara chose the middle name. He remains a handsome guy—he looks like a cross between young Orson Welles and Rainn Wilson—but was an extraordinarily beautiful baby. If they'd thought to do it, they could easily have hired him as a model for Gerbers. The photos of him are almost too perfect to be believed. Barbara was good with babies. She nicknamed her infant son "Luck Luck."

While the baby brought her joy, the birth itself was not lucky. Before, Barbara had had flights of eccentricity, but was able to keep it together. After, she could not. Something about the pregnancy and the birth triggered a change in her body chemistry. She was never quite the same after that. As her mental illness revealed itself, Frank had no idea what to do about it. What do you do when the woman you love, the mother of your son, is convinced that the license plates of the cars passing on the highway contained some sort of coded message that only she could decipher?

Nineteen sixty-six was a momentous year for the St. John family, and a perilous one for Barbara's mental health. She began working at Lycoming, in the purchasing department. Frank didn't see her during the day—they were in different departments—but they would commute to work together. Little Louis was watched by a woman in the neighborhood, herself a mother, who operated a de facto daycare from her house. When I asked after this woman, who must have been an important figure in his young son's life, Franklin could not remember her name.

In July of '66, Frank and Barbara took a month off from work and went to Europe—their first big trip. The vacation was paid for, he tells me, by the money Barbara earned at Lycoming. They went to Italy. They went to France.

"This was in '66?" I asked, puzzled. "Where was Louis?"

"Oh, he was with the same woman who took care of him."

Yes, things were different back then, but I can't even imagine leaving a 20-month-old in the care of *anyone* else for that long, much less a non-family member, while I went gallivanting around the Old Country. Why would they have even *wanted* to go away for so long? How could they have relaxed? What effect did it have on the young boy, not quite two, for his parents to suddenly vanish for four weeks? At that age, four weeks is an eternity.

As it happened, the trip was anything but relaxing. In Paris, Franklin went out for a walk after dinner, and came back to the hotel room to find Barbara at the desk, composing a love letter to another man—someone who worked with her in the purchasing department. This led to a volcanic row. He stormed out, and when he returned, she had snapped out of it. She was lucid again—as if the entire altercation never happened.

While Barbara was certainly flirtatious with other men, Frank doesn't know whether or not she followed through with her mental infidelities. On one occasion, a man he didn't know knocked on the door, and when Frank answered, the stranger shouted, "You keep your wife away from me!" That suggests that the love affair existed only in Barbara's mind. But a second alleged paramour was so often the topic of her conversation that Frank drove to his house to call him out. He found the man at dinner with his own wife. The guy's face went white when he opened the door.

"If you want her," Frank said, "she's in the car. Go and take her."

The man did not take him up on the offer.

If Frank entertained any notion of divorce, his religious upbringing quashed it. "If I wasn't Catholic, I don't know, maybe I would have left," he tells me.

Nineteen sixty-six was a bad year for the Powell family in general. Walter Powell, Barbara's oldest brother, was also in crisis. His wife, Eleanor, had left him, just walked out, leaving him with four young children—like in the Kenny Rogers song "Lucille." The poor guy was completely overwhelmed—heartbroken, but also ill-equipped to raise his young family all by himself. Her brother Richard came by one night and begged Frank and Barbara to take in Walter's youngest child, Alex, who was about the same age as Louis. Frank agreed. And for the rest of that year, and well into 1967, there were two young children in the house. Frank developed a strong bond with Alex. He offered to adopt him—and no sooner was that offer on the table when Walter came by to retrieve his young son.

It's instructive to look at 1966 from Barbara's housewife/young mother perspective. Her husband has a great career, but he's working almost all the time, whether at Lycoming or at a series of supplemental side hustles. She has a few friends from her younger days, but she's mostly alone with her toddler son.

She starts working at Lycoming, to get out of the house and alleviate her boredom. She begins at least one affair—whether in real life or in her own mind—with a co-worker there. This is interrupted by a four-week vacation in Europe, bookended by ocean voyages on the QE2. While in Paris, she has a sort of breakdown and is clearly thinking about her (real or imagined) lover back home—and not her young son. No sooner does she return from Europe than her brother drops off his own two-year-old boy for an indeterminate stay. She quits her job at Lycoming, and is suddenly home alone with her two-year-old son *and* her two-year-old nephew. She spends an inordinate amount of time at the kitchen table, chain smoking and drinking pots of black coffee. She's making lists. She's planning dinner recipes. She's trying to make sense of the coded messages she sees in the license plates. She's taking four or five different medications, including Haldol and Lithium, that put her, as Frank recalls, in a "zombie-like state." She doesn't like being a zombie, so she stops taking her medication. And then, just before Christmas of 1966, she snaps.

Frank cannot recall the name of the mental institute where he brought Barbara—only that it was Exit 18 off the Interstate. She'd been there before, a few times, the first in 1964, not long after Louis was born. But this time was different. "She was *out*," he recalls. "Gone." She would spend three full months at that facility, receiving treatment.

The night of Christmas, 1966, Franklin was home with Louis and Alex, the two-year-olds, and he was in tears. He was alone. He didn't know what he was going to do. The future terrified him. This was one of the lowest points of his life.

"I was not the best husband," he admits now. "I made a good living. But when you make a good living, sacrifices are made."

Despite all of the adversity in his home life, Frank went to work every day as if nothing was wrong. He compartmentalized like a champ. As soon as he walked through the door of the Lycoming building, he was fully in work mode. Incredibly, he did not mention the Barbara situation to anyone. Even his best friend, Walter Jensen, had no idea that anything was wrong.

11

STRANGE KARMA

Frank's career at Lycoming coincided with the escalation of the conflict in Vietnam. He started in the fall of 1962, right around the time of the Cuban Missile Crisis of October 16-28. The United States had taken over primary operations in what was once French Indochina after the humiliating French defeat at Dien Bien Phu in 1954. The region became the site of a proxy war between the U.S. and the Soviet Union. Our side had better ideas about freedom and democracy; the Communists, alas, had Võ Nguyên Giáp, one of the canniest military strategists of the twentieth century. In hindsight, the case for war seems silly, if not outright insane, but in 1962, with the Cold War in full swing, and both powers armed with enough nuclear weapons to destroy the earth a hundred times over, there was great enthusiasm for defending Vietnam from Communist incursion. A loss there would create a "domino effect," and we couldn't have *that*. First JFK, then LBJ, then Richard Nixon—two Democrats and a Republican—sent troops to Vietnam.

Although Franklin was of age for military service, his job at the plant was deemed vital to the war effort, so he was spared from the draft. And in his way, he did quite a bit for his coevals who were fighting in Vietnam.

By 1967, Frank was in charge of Quality Control and Production, overseeing a department of three engineers and a few dozen technicians. One of the former was a man named

Joe, who stood six-four barefoot and was made of muscle. Although not an old man, Joe's face was lined with rage and drink. Probably he didn't imbibe on the job, but in the mornings, he sweat out the booze from the night before, so he always had a faintly wino reek to him. Frank described him as having "little energy," which was probably attributable to the guy's daily hangover. As with the bragging bowler, he immediately took a dislike to him—and the feeling was mutual.

Shortly after his transfer to the new gig, bad news came in from Vietnam. Helicopter engines had failed in the field, causing the death of some soldiers. One imagines those metal birds fully formed, but they were built with parts manufactured in plants all around the country. The engine parts were made by Lycoming—in this case, at the company's plant in South Carolina. Frank got on a plane and flew down to the facility, to analyze the failed engines that had been shipped back from Saigon.

Right away he spotted the problem: the compressor section had failed on every one of the busted engines. His heart sunk in his chest. The fractured compressor blades had all been made in Connecticut. *His own division* had been responsible for an error that led to American soldiers dying. With heavy heart, he had the parts shipped back to Stratford, and returned home.

He invests a full page in his memoirs discussing the metallurgical problem he found. I'll try to do it justice here: Compressor blades spin furiously in the compressor, a part of the helicopter's engine that heats up to 1,200 degrees. To withstand those extreme conditions and not fail, the alloy used here is called AM-350, a combination of chromium, nickel, and molybdenum that is extremely resistant to corrosion.

After casting and forging, this type of steel is heated to 1,500-1,700 degrees Fahrenheit, and then quenched in liquid nitrogen, to get to 100 degrees below zero. When it is superheated, the alloy's structure is *face-centered cubic*, meaning that the atomic centers are arranged in such a way that one atom is located at each corner of a cube shape, with one also at the center of each face. This creates 14 identical lattice points. (Don't worry, I barely understand this, either). It looks like this:

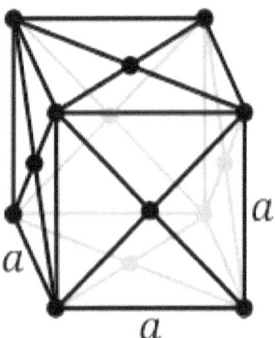

When the alloy is cooled, the atoms shift to a *body-centered cubic* arrangement, which, to the eyes of this writer, is a bit simpler in composition:

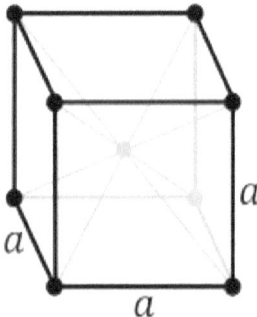

At room temp, the alloy arrays itself in the latter arrangement. But the cooling process is so rapid that, if not done properly, the structure gets caught in the middle—like an elevator that opens its door when it's between two floors. The result is an arrangement that is *body-centered tetragonal*:

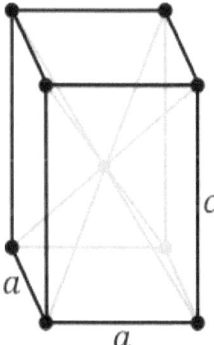

The structure is too hard, and too brittle, and thus cannot withstand the corrosion caused by the compressor; the chromium is tied up by the improper heat treatment, making the grain boundaries more susceptible to corrosion. AM-350 has to be tempered—that is, heated to about 1,000 degrees Fahrenheit. But, because of its unique composition, it does not achieve the body-centered tetragonal shape at room temperature. For that to happen—for the alloy to work properly—the metal must be cooled in liquid nitrogen to at least -100 degrees Fahrenheit. That doesn't sound like that big of a deal, but it's the difference between a helicopter engine that works and one that blows up somewhere over Dong Ha City.[2]

When he got the malfunctioning parts back to the Connecticut lab, Frank began his analysis of the failure. First he examined the fracture surfaces for evidence of fatigue failures, which would have indicated a flaw in the design of the engine. But there was no evidence of fatigue. Then he had sections of the blades mounted, polished, and etched for metallurgical examination. At 500 magnifications, he could see, plain as day, that there were basic structural problems with the alloy

---

[2] Frank says that my explanation here isn't perfect, but you get the idea.

itself—a result of an error in heat treatment. He found chromium carbides in the grain boundaries. To me, that sounds like gibberish, but to Frank, it revealed why the blades had failed: either the alloy had only been quenched to room temperature, or the quench itself had been interrupted. As a result of the error, the alloy was no longer resistant to corrosion. The chromium carbides messed that up. What this meant, in the grand scheme, was that when the engine of the chopper was fired up, and the internal temperature soared to some 1,200 degrees Fahrenheit, the blades corroded and, ultimately, failed. That's what happened to the engines of those helicopters in Vietnam.

With that mystery solved, Frank went to work on another: how on earth this shoddy alloy could have been approved and released to manufacturing in the first place. It was impossible to know for sure. Quality reports indicated that the flawed material had been approved. But not all of it was bad.

When the next batch of AM-350 came in, Frank tested it. And the one after that, and the one after that, and the one after that. The answer hit him one day when he came back from lunch to find eight new batches of AM-350 released for production. "I immediately stopped the release of the material," he recalls. "There's no way eight batches of *anything* could be properly examined in the 45 minutes I was at lunch."

The culprit turned out to be, you guessed it, his nemesis Joe, the drunk. Livid, Frank summoned him to his office and let him have it. Joe refused to back down. "Are you questioning my professional integrity? How dare you!" But Frank was right.

Because of union regulations at the time, the company could not immediately fire him. But there was a round of layoffs two weeks later, and Joe's name moved to the top of that list. When he was let go, he had one of his cronies deliver Frank a message: Joe was going to kick his ass! "Name the time and place," Frank shot back, "and I'll be there!" But the fight never materialized.

A few months later, Joe was killed in a single-car accident, probably while under the influence. The engineer responsible for those helicopter crashes in Vietnam was himself killed in a crash. As Frank wrote in his memoirs, "Strange karma!"

12

PRINCE OF ALL

BARBARA'S STRUGGLES WITH MENTAL ILLNESS continued throughout her life, but for nine or ten months in 1968-69, she was as lucid as she'd been in years. She stopped writing in her notebooks. She stopped seeing messages in license plates. She was back to the old Barbara Powell, the firecracker Frank had fallen head over heels for at the dance at the Polish Hall. What had been a marriage on the rocks suddenly and inexplicably righted itself.

Maybe it was the right combination of medications. Maybe Franklin spent more time at home, and that made things better. If you ask me, it was fate. Because if Barbara had not had this period of lucidity, and if the marriage had ended, my wife would never have been born, and I would not be writing this.

The story of her birth is one of the cornerstones of St. John family lore. Franklin enjoys telling it, and I've heard it hundreds of times: He is at work, as usual, on September 2, 1969, when he gets a call. His wife, who is eight months pregnant, has been in a car accident. He needs to get to the hospital at once.

When our son Dominick was born, my wife and I took weeks of childbirth classes. We hired a doula. I was with Stephanie in the hospital the entire time she was in labor—which wound up being well over 36 hours. There was never a question of whether we would be separated. Even when they did the C-section, I was right there, in scrubs and one of those silly medical hats, and I held my newborn baby boy before she got to.

Things were different in 1969. Expectant mothers were routinely separated from their husbands, who either paced in some waiting room, cigars at the ready, or else went home and waited for a phone call. So even if things had gone according to plan, Frank would not have been in the delivery room, holding his wife's hand. But this was different. The accident was not serious, and Barbara's injuries were minor. However, she was eight months pregnant, and the impact of the crash put the life of the baby at risk.

"I remember sitting in the waiting room," he recalls. "I said a prayer. I thought, 'Well, if the baby lives, it lives, and if it dies, it dies. There's nothing I can do about it.'" I think he likes this story because he gets to present himself as a man in charge of his emotions, even in his moment of adversity. My wife sees it differently. In her mind, he is "detaching," a common complaint she has about him, and how he copes with emotional trauma.

I'm pleased to report that the baby did survive. Aside from a crooked leg, which was adjusted with a brace, and a lazy eye, which years later was fixed with glasses and an eyepatch (much to her elementary-school chagrin), she was a healthy, happy, beautiful baby girl, with a radiant smile and gorgeous blue-green eyes. Barbara named her Stephanie, after Princess Stéphanie, daughter of Prince Rainier of Monaco and Grace Kelly. She called her Princess Stephanie, or Princess, or, eventually, Prince of All.

Barbara was good with babies and young children. She could be silly, and her sense of humor appealed to that demographic. She was always making up funny nicknames or sayings.

What she was not was a helicopter mom. One of Stephanie's earliest childhood memories is when she toddled into the bathroom, wriggled out of her cloth diaper, and disposed of the contents in the toilet, all by herself. It is cute to picture this happening, especially if you've seen photos of how adorable my wife was when she was two. But it speaks to a larger theme in her life: that she had to learn, from a very young age, to take care of herself.

13

ROVING INSPECTOR

LYCOMING MANUFACTURED ENGINES, but some of the raw material was provided by outside suppliers. Few outside suppliers had quality control like Lycoming did, because Franklin was very good at his job. When a problem came from one of the vendors, he was sent to inspect the outside facilities, to see if he could solve the problem. This happened when a shipment of SAE 4340 steel distorted during manufacture, shutting down production. Frank was dispatched to the supplier.

On the drive down, he thought through his knowledge of SAE 4340 steel. It was martensitic, he remembered; martensite, named for German metallurgist Alfred Martens, is an extremely hard form of carbon in iron that is a key component of hardened steel. (Martens, incidentally, despite being German, was not a Nazi; he died in 1914). That meant that the heat treatment had to be properly controlled, or the resulting steel structure might get wonky. But a company that manufactures steel would know that, surely.

Frank was met at the plant by the owner of the company. The two immediately hit it off. He can be a solitary fellow, not at all like his father, who was always the life of the party. But he could turn it on, channeling that Loosh energy, when it suited him. When he was off the clock, he was content to read, watch sports on TV, eat a nice meal, or other solitary pursuits. But when he was on the job, he became a veritable gameshow host.

He has a chameleon-like quality that allows him to adapt to the people around him. In a word, he's charming.

On this particular trip, both of Frank's two disparate skills—command of the arcane secrets of metallurgy, and the ability to charm the pants off someone—were on full display. First, he befriended the company owner. That was easy: second nature. Then he inspected the facility. This was a bit harder, but it didn't take him long to discover the problem.

The first thing Frank noticed when he walked into the heat treatment area was the placement of the quenching tanks, clear across the room from the heat treatment furnaces. He thought again about martensitic steel—that the heat treatment had to be properly controlled. Once the parts have been forged in the furnace, they must be immersed in water immediately.

He looked again at the furnace, and then at the quenching tanks. Then again at the furnace, and again at the quenching tanks. The owner of the company, looking at him, might have remarked that his head was on a swivel.

"The tanks," he said. "Move them next to the furnace."

And he explained how, because the super-heated metal was being conveyed across the room, the quench was not accomplished quickly enough.

"That's the problem."

The owner was so pleased—and, probably, embarrassed—that he took Frank to lunch. Over cheeseburgers, they shot the breeze. Frank mentioned that he had a side business selling wigs out of the back of his car. (*Why* he had a side business selling wigs, of all things, out of the back of his car, I have no idea, but he did). After work that day, the man took Frank to his house, where his wife and daughter each bought a wig and wiglettes. Whether they actually wanted the merchandise, or were making the purchases to stay in the good graces of the failure analyst from their largest customer, I have no idea. But Frank drove home with his mission accomplished, and extra money in his pocket to boot—not a bad haul after a day on the road. It would not be the last time that his blend of metallurgical know-how and natural-born salesmanship would reap profits.

In his work life, especially in the early years, Frank was blessed with good luck. In 1970, he left Lycoming for Huyck Metals. The job paid better and was also less than a mile from his house. He was fast-tracked to management, and on the first of the year, 1971, he was named assistant manager. All signs pointed toward another promotion in the near future—to Manager of Engineering. Huyck was a much smaller outfit than Lycoming, which only made the (vacant) position all the more prestigious. Things were looking up—until word came that most of the employees were being laid off, because Pratt Whitney, far and away their biggest customer, was no longer buying from them.

This meant Frank had to return, tail between his legs, to Lycoming. Fortunately, this was not hard. His old boss, Barry Goldblatt, had called him three or four times, imploring him to come back to his old stomping grounds. Frank turned him down each time, explaining that while he liked the place, it didn't offer him the best opportunity.

But now the situation had changed. "Barry," Frank said, calling him up, "I've got a wonderful metallurgist that I think you should hire immediately."

"Really? Who is he?"

"Me."

And so he was welcomed back, with open arms, to Lycoming. But he didn't stay long. About a year after his return, he was summoned to the office of his manager, the wonderfully-named Romeo Pappiro.

"What I'm about to tell you, it doesn't leave this room."

Frank nodded, agreeing.

"What do you know about Heppenstall."

"Not a thing."

"They're big steel manufacturers. They're based in Pittsburgh, but they have a satellite plant in Philadelphia. Midvale, it's called. My friend Joe Giacco—we grew up together—he's a big wheel in the main office. He says they need a chief metallurgist for the Philly location. And I thought of you."

"I don't know," he said. "I've never worked in steel."

"You'll pick it up quick enough. I'd hate to lose you, but Joe needs somebody good, somebody he can trust. And it's a step up for you."

Frank had Romeo set up the interview, and he was offered the job. Barbara wasn't crazy about moving, but Frank jumped at the opportunity. So after a few months of crazy commuting, the St. John family packed up and moved to the Keystone State.

Little did he know that he was leaving Connecticut Nazis to work for Philly mobsters.

PART THREE

PENNSYLVANIA

In Connecticut, ca. 1971, Estelle Powell with Stephanie;
Barbara is holding not one but two cats: Bob and Charlie.

14

NICETOWN STEEL

NICETOWN IS A BLUE-COLLAR NEIGHBORHOOD in North Philadelphia, not far from the Schuykill River. Bounded on the south by a massive tangle of railroad tracks, the place was a hub of manufacturing during the glory days of American industry. The giant Midvale Steel plant, smack dab in the center of the neighborhood, brought jobs to the inhabitants— and not just the white ones. Midvale was one of the first U.S. companies of its kind to recruit Black workers. The loss of manufacturing jobs was particularly devastating to Nicetown's African-American community. Race riots there, in the wake of the assassination of Martin Luther King, Jr. in 1968, scared off many white inhabitants—mostly Italians and Irish whose ancestors had labored at the factories a generation before. In the early 70s, when Franklin worked there, it was one of the poorest, sketchiest sections of the city.

Nicetown was anything but nice.

Midvale was, back in the Chester Arthur Administration, the employer of the great Frederick Winslow Taylor, who basically invented the concept of management consulting. His landmark work *The Principles of Scientific Management* is arguably the most influential management book of the twentieth century. With his Arrow collars, pomaded hair, and smart mustache, Taylor is one of those Progressive Era, Protestant-work-ethic dynamos that are now an easily mocked stereotype—the sort of old timey go-getter they make fun of on *The Simpsons*. In addition to founding the steel company, writing the book, doing management consulting, inventing industrial engineering, and playing competitive tennis and golf, he was a mechanical engineer by trade, who made piles of money patenting steel process improvements.

This was reflected at Midvale, a much smaller outfit than Carnegie, Bethlehem, or the behemoth U.S. Steel. The company made its mark by pioneering steel formulae used in the early days of the automotive industry—back when Carl Benz was still tinkering with new models. If the other companies could churn out steel on a giant scale, Midvale was more careful and deliberate—a concern that helped transform steelmaking from black art to applied science. During the Great War, Midvale churned out the so-called "Midvale Unbreakable"-capped projectiles for warships, which had the ability to pierce even the strongest armor. During the first half of the twentieth century, the company became the Krupps of the New World.

By 1956, however, its fortunes were in decline. Midvale merged with Heppenstall Steel of Pittsburgh. The executives were all in Steel City, not much interested in venturing to Nicetown.

When Franklin worked there, Midvale occupied some 80 acres abutting the railroad tracks that brought in raw materials and transported out its finished steel products. Rail tracks crisscrossed the acreage like veins, with flatbed cars yoked to locomotives, conveying impossibly heavy equipment and materials around the facility. It was as industrial as industrial can be. Some two dozen buildings, large and small, rose up around the tracks.

One was the Administration Building, which, as the name suggests, headquartered the company's administrative functions: purchasing, accounting, personnel, and the office of the general manager, one Ed Slocumb.[3] Slocumb was the head

---

[3]   Some of the names in the book have been changed.

of the Philadelphia facility and reported directly to the high-er-ups in Pittsburgh.

Another was the Melt Shop, with its 30-, 50-, and 100-ton furnaces constantly ablaze. Sometimes it took the power of all three furnaces to melt a single enormous ingot. The shop also boasted an induction furnace used to re-melt defective ingots, the better to skim off the impurities. Some days, Franklin saw wrecked automobiles, sent from the junkyards all around Eastern PA, fed directly into the furnaces. Anyone who has played with toy Matchbox cars can imagine such a scene, but the sheer scale of the operation, the weight and power of it, must have been breathtaking to behold—especially for a son of the Upper Peninsula of Michigan, where the largest object in the workplace was a log.

Ingots made their way from the Melt Shop to the Forge Shop, which also contained enormous furnaces that heated the steel enough for the ingots to be forged into specific shapes. Rolls for steel forming went to the Heat Treatment Building, where the eponymous heat treatment gave the material added strength, hardness, toughness, ductility, and corrosion resis-tance. A second Heat Treatment Building was for smaller products: disks, blades, shafts, pistons, and so forth. A third, called the High Building, had enormously tall furnaces designed to heat-treat shafts that were 50 feet long.

The last step of the manufacturing process was Machining, where the treated steel was cut into the final shapes and sizes. Even in 1972, Midvale had computer-operated equipment that could machine accurately to extremely close tolerances.

Last but not least was the small building that housed Metallurgy Quality Control. This is where Franklin, as Chief Metallurgist, punched the clock. His direct supervisor was a petty and insecure middle manager named Bill Gilson—a major character in St. John family lore.

15

FUCK YOU, GILSON

RIGHT OFF THE BAT, Frank knew Gilson would be a problem. Oh, the interview went well. Interviews always did. This was the era when scientists had crewcuts and square glasses and pocket protectors and the personalities of a lump of anthracite coal. Franklin was special, in that he could play with the egg-heads in that world, but also turn on enough winsomeness to charm the pants off anyone, scientist or otherwise.

Joe Giacco—the old friend of Romeo Pappiro, who'd recommended him for the job—participated in the interview. Joe was well-dressed, pleasant, smart, and already pre-disposed to like him. Frank and Joe clicked almost immediately. But the other man in the conference room of the Administration Building that day, the middle manager who oversaw operations in Philadelphia, would be his actual supervisor. Bill Gilson was cagey that day. He didn't have much to say. For much of the interview, his face bore an unusual expression that signified contempt, jealousy, an urgent need to move his bowels, or all three.

From what I can gather, Gilson was kind of a nebbish. He was seven years older than Frank and had been with the company for over a decade, diligently climbing up the man-agerial ranks. He was perfectly adept at doing the job he'd been trained to do, but lacked the imagination or the initiative to improve anything, or to adapt in any way to the changing times. He dressed like it was still 1955, and thought that way too. Midvale desperately needed a visionary in that role at that time, and Bill Gilson was no visionary. Frederick Winslow Taylor he was not.

Bill Gilson had a wife and kids and a mortgage. Bill Gilson had responsibilities. Bill Gilson had job stress—not least because his operation was hemorrhaging money, as we shall see. Bill Gilson was a staid, boring man who spent his free time leading a local Boy Scout troop. He had no sense of humor, and viewed outsiders as a threat. Certainly he viewed Franklin that way. Joe Giacco didn't drive from Pittsburgh to Philadelphia to tell Gilson, "This is Frank St. John. He's your replacement." But Gilson certainly interpreted it that way.

Whatever the reason, Gilson was a bad boss. He was petty and insecure. He sprung surprises on Frank for no good reason. He didn't have his back when he should have. He did nothing to train him or allow him to benefit from his decades of experience in steel. He was constantly putting him in a position to fail—and would then lose his temper when Frank would succeed despite the deck being stacked against him. As Gilson saw it, Frank was there to take his job as manager, and he was going to do everything in his power to stop that from happening.

A once-proud company, Midvale was now a mess. To call the facility a "disaster area" would not even be hyperbole. Frank was used to working for companies run by ex-Nazis, with stereotypical German efficiency. This place, unlike Lycoming, was falling apart. And it was dangerous. Workers were constantly getting hurt on the job because the conditions were woeful. Not only that, but there were urgent problems that needed fixing. Like the technicians in Machining, the Chief Metallurgist had his work cut out for him.

Tensions with the dour, sour-pussed Gilson soon came to a head. Six months or so after Frank started at Midvale, there was a serious problem with shafts that the company was manufacturing for General Electric—one of its biggest and most important clients. These were enormous cylinders of steel, 50 feet long and 12 feet in diameter. And now 20 of them had to be scrapped for failing tests for hardness and tensile strength. This was an enormous waste of raw materials, and a potential disaster for the bottom line.

At the end of the day, just as he was about to go home—to a house he'd only lived in for a month or so, when he finally moved Barbara and the kids to Pennsylvania—Frank was summoned to Administration, to see Bill Gilson.

"We have a serious problem," his boss snarled, ignoring any pretense of pleasantries. "Or, should I say, *you* have a serious problem. After all, *you're* the Chief Metallurgist." The contempt in his voice was impossible to conceal.

"Oh, yeah? And what problem is that?"

And Gilson explained about the failure of the GE shafts. "That's big money. And it happened on your watch. I wonder what your buddy Joe will think when he sees how badly you bungled things."

"Those GE shafts," Frank shot back, "were made and shipped out before I started working here."

"Were they? Don't be so sure. In any case, what does it matter? You're the one in charge of Metallurgy, so I'll make damned sure they know where the buck stops."

"Go to hell."

He thought about slugging Gilson in the mouth—Gilson was, I'm told, cursed with a singularly punchable face—but instead, he marched out of the office, slamming the door behind him. As he was racing down the stairs, he could hear his boss ordering him to come back. Frank paused for a split second, exhaled, and kept right on going.

When he got home, he kissed Barbara on the cheek. He tried to tamp down his rage but couldn't. So he changed into his sweats and sneakers and went to the nearby high school, where there was a track around the football field. He ran a mile, then another, then another. Only when he was completely exhausted, his rage finally spent, did he come home for dinner.

He drove to Nicetown the next day convinced he'd get fired. The only way he could have been more insubordinate was to slug the guy in the jaw—and he came *this close* to doing that! Sure enough, as soon as he walked in the door, word came that he was to report to Administration at once.

"Oh, well," Frank thought. "It was fun while it lasted."

But Gilson was serene. He even managed to smile, although the effort seemed to cause him great pain. "You know," he said, "after our...*discussion* yesterday, I was very upset. But when I got home, I took my son to a Boy Scout meeting. It was nice. It really calmed me down and made me feel better."

"That's terrific, Bill," Frank said. "I'm so happy to hear that. Me, when I got home, I went for a run."

"Oh, that's good. Very good. Exercise is good for relaxation."

"It really is. Especially the way I do it."

"And what way is that?"

"I run around the track as fast as I can, and every time my foot hits the ground, I say, 'Fuck you, Gilson. Fuck you, Gilson.'"

Poor Gilson had no idea how to process this. Here the poor guy had made every effort to make the peace, only to have Franklin throw it back in his face, as vulgarly as possible. He didn't know what to say. So he burst out laughing—a rare occurrence. Frank laughed, too.

And no, this was not the beginning of a beautiful friendship. Frank never took to Gilson, and Gilson continued to treat him with open hostility.

The story of the track is one of Frank's all-time favorites—so much so that when I researched Bill Gilson for the book, and came across his obituary on a site where loved ones can connect over deceased friends and relations, I had to resist leaving a comment that just said, "Frank St. John says fuck you, Gilson."

16

BERWYN

ALTHOUGH SHE HAD BRISTLED AT THE IDEA, Barbara wound up loving Pennsylvania. For the first time in her life, she'd put some distance between herself and her troubled family. Her overbearing, cuckolded mother; her alcoholic, suicidal little brother; her broken older brother, whose wife abandoned him with their four kids—all of that was left behind in Connecticut, a four-hour car ride away. In the days before social media and cell phones, when long-distance phone bills were extravagantly expensive, they may as well have lived on another planet. Far way, too, were her lovers, real or imagined, from her stint at Lycoming. If anyone needed a fresh start in another state, it was Barbara Powell.

Berwyn is a quaint, charming town in Chester County, on the Philadelphia Upper Main Line. It has a train station that looks like something out of Walt Disney World. It has a vibrant community theater. It has a vast public park donated by the investment-banker brother of painter Mary Cassatt. It is the home of presidential power couple David Eisenhower and Julie Nixon Eisenhower. It is the American dream small town.

In St. John family lore, Berwyn is a special, almost magical place. Louis was seven, my wife was two when they moved there. For Stephanie, recollections of that house comprise her earliest childhood memories. I asked her to write about her recollections. This is what she turned in:

I remember it was a rainy day, and we walked into the house through the bottom level, which was in the back of the house facing the backyard. I was with my mom, my dad, and my brother—which in and of itself was a special occasion, given that on most Saturdays Dad was not around. We pushed open the screen door revealing a group of blonde- haired kids, all different sizes and ages, all quiet, sitting on the couch, on the floor, all enraptured by the television which was playing *The Brady Bunch*. A 1970s family of blonds watching a 1970s family of blondes (and ok, brunettes if you count Mike, Bobby, Greg, and Peter.) They all looked at us at the same time, like crabs awakened on a beach, and then quickly turned back to the TV. That's what I remember from seeing the house that we would eventually buy and move into a few months later. We were moving to Pennsylvania—or how I said it: *Pencil-AY-nee-uh*. Our split-level house had a red door. My mom would sing the Rolling Stones song about how he sees your red door and he wants to paint it black. I really hoped that wouldn't be the case, as I really liked that door.

I really liked our house. Through the front door, you had a choice of going upstairs or downstairs. Going up, you would have a bee-line right into the kitchen, which had a pass-through with, get this, little shutters you could latch and close, so if you were cooking you could have a little privacy from the dining room. To the left of the stairs was the living room and then the dining room, which was also to the left of the kitchen. If you took a right from the stairs you'd go up five or six carpeted steps to the three bedrooms and bathroom. I had my grandmother's old bed-set, so I had a big giant bed all to myself. My brother's room was on the right. Mine was in the middle at the end of the hall, and my parents was to the left. They had their own bathroom. I remember going in to wake up my mom if she was still sleeping and I needed breakfast. I also remember changing my own cloth diaper and flushing it by accident down the toilet—another reason to go in and wake my mom. Other times, if I were hungry, I'd just go rummaging through the cabinets and have at it with whatever I'd find. Legend has it that during one of my mom's naps, the one during the day that I would take with her, I woke up and left her there sleeping to go buck-wild with the treats I found in the kitchen cabinets. There were bites taken out of several Ring Dings and smooshed Ding Dong and Devil Dogs remains all over the kitchen counter and cabinets. Who could blame me?

Maybe I look back on the Berwyn time as the last time I felt like a normal family. Maybe that's why I love split-level houses. While my brother was at school and my Dad was at work, I'd spend my days watching PBS in the "red room," which was the uppermost level of the split level. It had red carpeting, hence its name. My mom would sit on the couch behind me smoking while I sat on the floor learning how to read and count from *Sesame Street*, and that I was great just the way I was from Mr. Rogers. There were days that we would leave the house to go places like the grocery store and the fabric store. I loved the fabric store. The big giant spools of fabric to make dresses with! I remember talking to the sales lady as my mom looked around and telling her that I could count to 70. And she patiently listened to me as I counted very slowly to 70. I must have made a mistake somewhere because I distinctly remember her saying, "I think it's 60 that comes next." I still can hear her voice say 60 in a very 1970s woman way: *see-ix-teee*.

Sometimes we'd go to some kind of mall that had these giant blue and green dinosaurs that you could climb on. I often think of these places as these mythical, mystical places. What I would give to see those dinosaurs now. To me, they were magic. Dinosaurs inside that you could climb on. I think I was the kind of kid that was ok being "free range." I still operate that way. Do not pay too much attention to me and let me do my thing. But I guess I started to become trouble. Like the time I ran out of the house naked, and my mom had to chase me down the street. I also ran up and down the aisles at church. Yes, we went to church sometimes. But not very much—refer to last sentence for why. I had three friends: Tonya, Margaret, and Elizabeth. They each came to my fourth birthday party. Everyone dressed up in sun dresses and hats. My mom actually took a bunch of pictures. I wore my special purple checked ruffly dress that you can see in my Sears Portrait Studio picture. The party was a great time. And I have the pictures to prove it! Tonya was the best friend out of the three. She lived with her grandparents, Mudsy and Harriet. How can you forget names like that? I obviously liked going to their house because one day, without telling anyone, I left our house and walked right into theirs. Which I'm guessing wasn't too far of a walk from ours. I realized that maybe I shouldn't have done that as it started to feel weird that it seemed like no one was home. I heard some voices and instead of leaving the house, I ran and hid behind one of their big, upholstered dining room chairs. I hid there for a while not knowing what to do as they started to get dinner ready and put food on the table. As dinner got closer, I couldn't take it anymore and I stood up and started crying. They brought me back to my house. I guess it was an odd thing to do. But what did I know? I think I wanted to stay there. I did like Mudsy and Harriet. And Tonya. I never knew why she lived with her grandparents and not her parents.

My mom also told me that one day, I locked her out of the house. Not sure how we resolved that one. And one time while shopping, I hid in one of those circular jeans racks. And when I was done hiding, I could not find my mom. I went up to the sales clerk behind the counter and said, "My mom is lost." They all thought that was funny. Even Mom. It became one of those stories that you tell for years. How clever I was to phrase it that way. But hey, my mom *was* lost.

So after a while, I became "too much" for my mom to handle so I started to go to a preschool or day care. The first day care I went to did not go well. I brought my blanket, my prized possession (I still mourn the loss of my blanket which happened at my brother's little league game later on in Connecticut). These little girls at the daycare wanted my blanket and took it from me. So I got upset and kicked them because they wouldn't give it back. When my mom came to pick me up, they said I was unruly, rude, something like that. It was not positive. And I remember feeling really wronged. Like those girls took my blanket. Um. Not ok! But who got in trouble? Me. I guess I didn't have people skills yet. I don't think I went back there. Nowadays I would have been the kid with ADHD. And I really would have, as I've been diagnosed with adult ADD. It all makes sense now. I am not to be boxed in, then or now.

We had two cats: Bob and Charlie. Bob was mine. He used to sleep in the crib with me back in Orange, Connecticut. Charlie was my mom's. He only loved my mom. As in he *hated* my dad. Because my dad was not a natural cat person. More of a dog guy. We cat people know that you need to let the cats come to you and choose you. That was not my dad's alpha style.

My mom would sew little hats for the cats. She'd make someone take a picture of her holding the cat while it was wearing the humiliating hat. Charlie put up with it because he truly loved my mom. Charlie and Bob did not get along (Charlie was kind of an asshole.) One day we got a dog named Patrick. He was crazy. He ate through tin cans and was pretty hard to handle. Legend has it that we were all out in the yard one sunny Sunday, and Bob came up to me, rubbed up against my leg and walked under the wooden fence and through the bushes away from our house. I said to everyone, "Bob's going on 'cation!"

And he never came back. He never, ever returned. I think Patrick the dog sent Bob over the edge. He was done. And I called it. Redrum!

The years in Pennsylvania were the happiest in the St. John annals. As you can see, Stephanie regards that period with reverence bordering on the mythological. And I can understand why. The house was handsome, the town was lovely, and the four of them—Frank, Barbara, Louis, Stephanie, plus whatever pets they owned at the time—functioned well as a nuclear family. For that finite, and too short, period of time, Franklin was not working crazy hours, and Barbara's demons were kept in check.

Stephanie and Louis both have an outsized fondness for *The Brady Bunch*, and I think part of it is because that show evokes memories of their own childhood in Berwyn at that time—a period when their mother and father could compete as ideal parents with Mike and Carol Brady (who, come to think of it, bear more than a passing resemblance to early- 70s Frank and Barbara St. John).

17

TROUBLE AT THE HIGH BUILDING

WHETHER the miscommunication was ultimately Bill Gilson's fault or Frank's, the General Electric account really was in jeopardy. The blue-chip corporation put the kibosh on all shipments from Midvale until the manufacturing problems were solved. This had the potential to sink the entire company. GE, as discussed, was Midvale's biggest and most important customer.

The buck stopped with Ed Slocumb, Sr., who after all was the general manager of the Nicetown facility, at least on paper. But he made damned sure that Joe Giacco and the big boys in Pittsburgh knew that Gilson was on the job, and Gilson, in turn, made certain that everyone knew he'd assigned the task to Franklin.

For Gilson, this was a win-win. If Frank figured out the problem, great—that would reflect well on the manager who knew to give him the assignment. And if he didn't solve the problem, well, Gilson could complain to Pittsburgh that the new guy, the arrogant whippersnapper with the foul mouth, had failed and should therefore be fired. Either way, Gilson's ass was covered.

For Franklin, the pressure was on.

As soon as he drew the assignment, Frank went to the High Building, where the faulty GE shafts had been heat treated. The building was named for the size of its furnaces, which soared 60 feet into the air. But judging by the behavior of the people working there, the structure might as well have been called that because all the technicians seemed stoned.

The High Building was one of the oldest structures on the campus, built around the time of the Civil War. The bricks were crumbling. The paint was cracking. It was poorly lit and poorly ventilated. And no one who worked there seemed to give a shit. Climbing the steel spiral stairs that ringed the cylindrical furnaces, Frank came upon layers of cardboard and blankets, where sleepy, slothful technicians caught some shut-eye during second and third shift. The place had all the professionalism of an opium den.

The steel stairs gave way to a succession of platforms, three in all, where the temperature and fuel controls were located. It was on these platforms that the makeshift cots were arranged. Inspecting the controls, Frank noticed something strange—on the first platform, there was a torch next to the thermocouple. (Thermocouples, I should add—because, while I'd heard that word before, I didn't know what it meant—are thermoelectric gauges that measure temperature.)

Frank glanced at the operator, who was fidgeting uneasily. "Get rid of that thing."

"What, the torch?"

"Yes, the torch."

"I can't do that."

"What do you mean, you can't do that?"

"Without the torches, the recording instruments go out of whack."

"Out of whack?"

"Yeah."

"Wait, do you mean you *heat* the *thermocouple* with the *blowtorch*?"

"How else would I get it to work?"

Frank opened his mouth to speak, but no words came out. He couldn't believe what he had discovered. Instead of heating the furnace, where these precision shafts were being made, the technicians were heating…*the thermocouple*. No wonder everything was screwed up!

After the torch was removed, the problem was easy to spot. The thermocouples showed the heat of the furnace in the lower section was anywhere from 700 to 900 degrees—nowhere near the 1200 degrees necessary to properly heat-treat the shafts. At that temperature, Frank knew, the lower sections of the steel shaft would be too hard, and the top sections too soft, owing to the heat rising. That was why they were defective.

He looked around the place again: the sleepy operators, the checked-out technicians. Was he really the only person in the High Building who knew about the temperatures for heat-treating steel? Who were these boobs?

While he wanted to tell Gilson the news—or bypass Gilson and call Joe Giacco directly—the thermocouples were only half of the problem. The other issue was that, like a bathtub when you add hot water, the temperature was not consistent. The top half of the upright furnace was too hot, and the bottom half, not hot enough. Frank wanted to solve the whole puzzle before reporting on his progress.

So: how to adjust the gas flow so that a consistent, proper temperature was maintained in each furnace? This was more difficult than throwing away some torches and re-training the control operators.

The first step was to get accurate temperature readings. He purchased a bunch of electrical controllers, and set about installing them. To place them just so, he had to climb to the very top of the upright furnace, 60 feet off the ground. Looking down, he was overcome by a sudden rush of vertigo. He almost fainted, and lost his balance. If the operator high atop the furnace had not grabbed him, Frank would have fallen into the thing, and, as he put it in his memoirs, "You would not be reading this."

For two full weeks, he kept constant and careful track of the temperature readouts, adjusting the gas just so. He practically slept in the High Building—the cardboard boxes and blankets must have looked tempting at three in the morning. But by the end of his round-the-clock fortnight of hell, Frank had the furnaces running properly.

Not only that—he realized that, while the giant GE shafts were defective, they could be salvaged. They wouldn't have to be completely scrapped. Under his careful watch, each shaft was heat-treated, this time with precision, and shipped back out to General Electric. "As a conservative estimate," Frank says with pride, almost 50 years later, "I saved the company well over a million dollars."

He also saved the GE account.

Gilson was not pleased. He'd have preferred that Frank failed, even if that meant the loss of the General Electric account. He was short-sighted, and his professional jealousy outweighed the truth: had Frank not saved the day, the plant, and his job along with it, would have gone away. Instead, the GE people were over the moon.

18

FLY EAGLES FLY

It wasn't just Midvale whose ass Frank saved. General Electric itself was dramatically impacted by the loss of the shafts. One imagines a mighty enterprise like GE to be impervious to the failures of one of its many suppliers, but this was not the case. As the GE account manager remarked to Franklin, "You know, we expected to be out eight, nine months...maybe even a full year. Instead, we were only down a month."

To celebrate the job well done, the accounts guy took Frank, Bill Gilson, Ed Slocumb, and some of the other Midvale executives and managers to Veterans Stadium, where from a swanky luxury box, they watched the Eagles play football.

Frank is a big sports fan. He's not old enough to have watched Ty Cobb play, but his father did, and he's rooted for the Detroit Tigers since the halcyon days of Al Kaline and Hammerin' Hank Greenberg—who hit a whopping 58 home runs the year Frank was born. He loves basketball, particularly college basketball; in his retirement, he became an obsessive fan of the powerhouse UConn Women's Basketball Team, which during that stretch produced some of the finest players the sport had ever seen—including arguably *the* best, Diana Taurasi. He also likes football, but, like most fans of the Detroit Lions, he approaches that sport with pessimistic detachment, as his team hasn't been any good since trading its star quarterback, Bobby Layne, to the Steelers after winning the championship in 1958.

So it was with great delight that he took in the Eagles game that rollicking Sunday afternoon. Frank is not a drinker, as we have seen, but he allowed himself to join the fun, throwing back some cold beers with the GE accounts man and the rest of the guys in the booth. His best friend at Midvale was there, a genial fellow named Harvey Wynne, who handled the impossible task of quality control.

During the breaks in the action, Frank held court, telling and re-telling the tale of how he saved the day at the High Building. The GE guy, who was quite drunk, couldn't get enough of the story. Gilson laughed along with the others, but it was obvious to Frank, and to his friend Harvey Wynne, that there was no mirth beneath that laugh. "Poor Gilson! He expected that I would screw it up," he recalled, "because he gave me no help or direction concerning the problem. This really reflected poorly on him."

The party included someone Frank did not know very well. His name was Duquesne, and he ran the Maintenance Department. He was a mountain of a man, with a crooked nose, and a Habsburg jaw. His arms hung past his knees like an orangutan's. He looked like he could have thrown on a uniform and played a few downs at linebacker. At one point, Frank noticed him hobnobbing with Slocumb.

"Mr. St. John," he said, extending his big, powerful mitt, "I don't believe we've had the pleasure. I'm Mr. Duquesne."

"Hello." Frank extended his normal-sized hand, which the behemoth proceeded to crunch in his powerful grip.

"So you're the big hero who got the High Building operating again." Was it the booze talking, or was that contempt Frank detected in the thick Philly-accented voice? But why would anyone be *upset* that the problem was solved? Duquesne squeezed one last time on the captive hand, and it was all Frank could do not to yelp. "It's so great," he said, barely disguising the sarcasm, "to put name to face."

Frank realized that Duquesne was very drunk.

"Two million bucks."

"Pardon?"

"Two million bucks down the tubes."

Just then, the crowd went wild. The Eagles tailback had burst through a seam in the defense, juked out two defenders, and was taking it to the house. Duquesne released his grip to watch the play. Frank reclaimed his hand and retreated to the far corner of the room, where his friend Harvey was availing himself of another Labatt's.

"I don't think Duquesne likes me very much."

"Duquesne doesn't like anybody. Best to keep your distance."

"Yeah, I figured that out all on my own."

"I mean it. He's cousins with Little Nicky Scarfo or something."

"Little Nicky Scarfo. Does he work in Maintenance, too?" Harvey laughed.

"I'm serious. I have no idea who that is."

"He's Angelo Bruno's righthand man. But you probably don't know who that is, either."

"Does he play for the Eagles?"

Again, Harvey laughed. He had a good laugh, jolly and infectious. "I mean it. Stay away from Duquesne."

"I'm a quick study, Harvey. You don't have to tell me twice."

19

ROLLS

FOR HIS NEXT TRICK, Frank was tasked by Gilson—who, like a comic book villain, seemed to delight in putting him in increasingly-more-challenging situations—with figuring out the processing problem with cracked ingots. The sour-pussed manager was convinced that this was the thing that would foil the Chief Metallurgist—but Frank had a trick up his sleeve.

Unlike steel, which he did not work with until coming to Midvale, the ingots were made of Hastelloy X, a nickel alloy—a material he'd had hands-on experience working with since 1960. Even so, the issue was harder to solve that the GE shaft error. A routine check of the furnace confirmed that everything was in working order. His initial theory was that the ingots had spent too much time out of the furnace on each pass, with the temperature on the final pass being a touch too cold, causing the failure. To test this theory, Franklin used his trusty optical pyrometer, an instrument calibrated to match the color of radiation from the ingots to certain temperatures—an infrared thermometer, basically. (The ones they make now look like the doohickeys used to check if you have a fever before entering a doctor's office.)

Under Frank's careful supervision, the technicians worked the alloy. At the first sign of heat loss, he had them throw the ingots back in the furnace. The workers were none too pleased at having to constantly take the ingots in and out—it made the process take significantly longer—but Franklin insisted.

The process took 40 hours—almost two full days. He stayed in the plant the entire time. He had no choice—the workers simply didn't care about quality control. They were union workers, they couldn't be fired, and they had little financial incentive to do a good job. Frank failed to get through to them. "How do you get people to take pride in producing a quality product?" he wondered. But after the 40 hours of hell, the problem was solved. The ingots were perfect. The failure was corrected, the problem solved.

Foiled again, Gilson!

What's remarkable about this story is not that Frank fixed the problem. It's that he didn't bother to inform his wife of his whereabouts. He went into Work Mode for 40 hours, and only when he emerged did he realize he should have given her some advanced notice. When Barbara saw him, she was shocked. He looked like shit: unshaven, mussed hair, wrinkled clothes. He stank of sweat and the forge. He had a bit to eat and went to bed, but it took him a long time to fall asleep.

After a year on the job, Frank had analyzed, and fixed, most of the metallurgical failures. He'd saved the GE account. He'd finetuned the manufacture of the nickel-alloy ingots. The problems with the shafts and the blades were fixed. Two-thirds of the profits were generated in the sides of the business Frank had smoothed over.

Now he turned his attention to the other third—the most mysterious part of the company.

Rolls used in the manufacture of sheet metal occupied a designated area in the facility, and for some territorial reason Frank could never quite divine, was kept separate from the rest of the Midvale plant—like a gated community. But there were strange stories about the operation, and the questionable practices concerning how the rolls were made and sold. He and his friend Harvey Wynne, the quality control manager, decided to take a closer look.

Had he not done so, the entire history of the St. John family would be very different.

Like the High Building, the conditions inside the facility were astonishingly bad. Makeshift rest areas fashioned from cardboard boxes and old rags. Spills and leaks. Poor ventilation. Operators and technicians literally asleep at the switch. Worse, the finished product was faulty. As with the High Building, the technicians were lazy about maintaining the furnaces at the proper temperatures, leading to fluctuations in the heat of the furnace, leading to bad steel.

"I don't understand it," Frank said to Harvey. "With all the mistakes they're making, the finished product should fail more often than not."

"It doesn't."

"Really?"

"Nope. Not that *I've* heard about. And I'm the QC guy, I'd know. We don't get any complaints from customers. Never, not once."

Frank shook his head. "That doesn't make a lick of sense."

"Nothing about this place does," laughed Harvey.

"We should figure this out. Let's do a little cost analysis."

"Sure."

As Harvey collected the data, Frank kept up his inspections. He'd show up in the roll building at odd times, to try and catch them napping. To thwart this, the lollygagging workers developed an elaborate "early warning" system. They labored much harder on this than doing their actual jobs.

If the behavior of the employees puzzled him, the initial cost analysis only confused him further. "When you price a product," he told me, "you start with the cost of raw material, followed by labor costs, then overhead, and finally your profit margin. Harvey got the pricing of the final product and found that the selling price to the customers just barely covered the cost of material!" This was like buying a can of Coke for a dollar and selling it for 75 cents. Not only was the math screwy, but the business model was unsustainable. At some point, the revenue from the profitable parts of the company would not be sufficient to cover the vast losses from the lazy-bones outfit making rolls.

"We have to take this to Slocumb."

"I don't know, Frank."

"The company is losing God knows how much money every year. He needs to know."

"Maybe," Harvey said quietly, after a long pause, "he already knows?"

But Frank was already out the door and on his way to the general manager's office in the Administration Building. He knew he was right, and he knew that Slocumb needed to be briefed. It was the only way to save the company from going under.

As he opened the door to the waiting room, where the secretaries sat, the first person he saw was the linebacker-sized Duquesne, with his crooked nose and his scowl. He recognized Frank, narrowing his eyes in a menacing, Clint Eastwood kind of way. When Frank moved aside to let him through, Duquesne dropped his shoulder, making contact intentionally.

"Nice to see you, too, Duquesne."

Slocumb was behind his desk, poring over a crisp *Philadelphia Inquirer*. He seemed mildly annoyed, but then, he always seemed that way. While he was not as overt in his contempt as Gilson, the general manager never seemed to take kindly to the brash, arrogant chief metallurgist.

"What can I do for you, Frank?"

And with great excitement, Franklin shared his great discovery: the roll manufacturing operation was costing the company money. Every shipment that went out put a dent in the bottom line. The solution was either to cut the work-force—impossible, given union regs—or raise the price of the product. If the change wasn't made, and made fast, Midvale was on a collision course with Chapter 11.

"My recommendation," he said, sliding the report across the desk, "is to shut down the roll manufacturing department immediately."

Slocumb took up the papers. He looked down at them. He looked at Frank. He looked down at the papers. Then he tore them up and threw them in the trash.

"Now you listen, and you listen good," he said. "Midvale has been in the roll business for almost 100 years, and our customers expect us to be in this business, and we will be in this business for the foreseeable future."

"Not at this rate."

"Excuse me?"

"Nothing."

"Good. Now get out!"

Frank stumbled out of the general manager's office like a drunk leaving the bar after last call. He couldn't believe what had just happened. Nor could he come up with a reason why Slocumb had reacted so strangely. (In fact, I was the one who explained what was going on—40-some-odd years later—but we'll get to that shortly.)

20

GOLD PARACHUTE

IN 1968, WHILE STILL AT LYCOMING, Frank and his friend Walter Jensen, a brilliant technician with an inventive mind, had a conversation that would change the course of both of their lives. The previous evening, Jensen had dinner with his neighbor, Gordon Katz, and Katz's father, Leon. The former, a pathologist, was a recent med school graduate; the latter owned a thriving dental practice. Leon Katz, Frank found out, had started a side business selling gold alloys to other dentists. Nowadays, the manufacture of bridges and crowns is generally outsourced, but in 1968, most dentists produced them in house, in their own laboratories. They therefore needed suppliers for gold, one of the few metals that can be used for bridges and crowns. Katz's new enterprise eliminated the middleman, selling directly to other dentists. But he was having problems with Stern Gold, the wholesale vendor who produced the gold alloys for his operation. Stern was putting the squeeze on him, jacking up the prices. Their motive in asking Walter Jensen to the dinner was to talk him into setting up a manufacturing facility to make gold alloys. This way, Stern Gold could be cut out of the process altogether. Leon Katz offered Jensen fifteen grand a year plus a 25% ownership stake in the company—a very generous package.

"I don't know if I should do it," Walter said.

"Why on earth not?"

"I don't know that much about metallurgy."

"You'll figure it out."

"I don't know."

"You're making, what, ten grand a year now?"

"Nine point five."

Franklin fixed a look on his friend that I've seen often. His eyes squinted, his head cocked to the side, his mouth curled up. It was his way of saying, "Come on, man. Are you crazy?"

Walter took the job. In the early goings, he enlisted Franklin's help in testing the various alloys. In fact, Frank's very first company, St. John Laboratories, was established for the occasion. The company folded once the testing was complete. "If we ever need a metallurgist," Walter said, "I'll poach you."

Walter went to work for Leon Katz, and did pretty well for himself, and Franklin forgot all about that discussion—until Walter Jensen came to visit in September of 1973, right after his ill-fated meeting with Mr. Slocumb.

"How are things here? You like it?"

And Frank told his friend about the petty Bill Gilson, the lazy High Building technicians, the inept Mr. Slocumb.

"Sounds like you could use a change. As it happens, Dr. Katz is looking to hire a new metallurgist. He wants to meet with you."

"No kidding?"

"No kidding."

"I'll think about it."

And that's when there was an accident in the High Building. As discussed, the 60-foot-high tanks contained oil, which was used to quench the steel shafts. As Franklin went into the building one afternoon to inspect the premises, he heard a commotion—workers yelling and screaming and running, full speed, this way and that.

A worker had fallen into one of the tanks.

Incredibly, there was no railing around the hole, and he had slipped—probably on a patch of oil—and fallen. Sometimes the tanks were half-full of oil, sometimes they were completely empty. In 30 feet of oil, the man would have drowned, because you can't swim in oil. In an empty tank, he would have pancaked on the bottom and died from the impact. There was 10 feet of oil on that day—enough to soften his fall, but not enough that he couldn't bounce off the bottom and not drown. Also, the oil was not boiling hot—another stroke of luck.

As Frank came inside, a quick-thinking crane operator was lowering his attachment into the hole, to retrieve the fallen man, who had managed to grab hold of the air-line, the equivalent of the rogue weed the hero in every action movie seizes just before he falls off the cliff. Frank watched in amazement as the crane operator plucked the terrified, oil-drenched worker out of the tank—like a child extracting a stuffed animal from the glass container at the arcade.

This was an accident, that's all it was—but it was preventable. Midvale simply did not prioritize workplace safety. In 1973, OSHA spent two weeks at the facility and issued a staggering 1,108 safety violations. Frank didn't work 24/7 by the furnaces like the technicians and operators, but he spent enough time there to be at risk.

He thought about Jensen's proposal, about Dr. Katz's desire to meet. He went back to his desk. He placed a call to Connecticut and set up the interview.

Dr. Katz had a magnanimous, winsome personality. He was nothing like the dour Gilson or the condescending Slocumb. Franklin turned on the charm.

"How much are they paying you at Midvale?"

They were paying him $17,700. So without a moment's hesitation, Frank said, "$19,900."

"I wouldn't want you to come and make less than what you make now."

After negotiating health insurance for his family, Frank asked Dr. Katz to mail him an offer letter. Then he drove back to Philadelphia and went back to work.

21

· · · · · · · · · · · ·

BUST OUT

· · · · · · · · · · ·

Soon after his return from the interview, Harvey Wynne, the quality control guy who was Frank's best friend at Midvale, came to his office with a stack of documents. He'd finished his forensic analysis of the roll manufacturing operation.

"It's dirty," he said. "They're crooks."

"Yeah?"

"Midvale sends the rolls out to be machined by a vendor, right? Well, guess who gets a kickback on that transaction? The purchasing manager, and, you guessed it, Mr. Slocumb."

"No kidding."

"Slocumb won't shut down the roll manufacturing. What does he care if the company tanks? He's making money hand over fist!" Harvey was excited, and maybe a bit nervous. "Not only that, but your friend Duquesne? He had a vendor all lined up to replace the furnaces you fixed—and was slated to make a nice little kickback for himself."

Frank recalled Duquesne's drunken muttering at the Eagles game about the two million dollars. Now it made sense.

"You fucked that guy good."

"Couldn't happen to a nicer fellow."

"Christ," he said, "I need a cigarette."

Frank didn't like smoking, but he allowed it this time.

"What should we do?"

"Not a thing," Frank said. "Not a damn thing. One minute you figure this all out, the next minute they're fishing your body out of the Schuylkill River."

Harvey, inhaling, coughed.

"Look, I'm leaving soon."

"Yeah?"

"I'm taking a job in Connecticut. I'm getting out of here. I suggest you do the same."

The formal offer came in the mail. Frank replied with his formal acceptance, pledging to begin in January. He gave notice in December. Gilson could barely contain his glee; it was the only time in Frank's entire stint at Midvale when his petty supervisor was actually nice to him.

Joe Giacco, in Pittsburgh, was less enthused. He begged him to reconsider, but Frank refused. He thought about telling Giacco about the kickbacks, but decided it was too risky.

Some of the technicians and operators were sad to see him go. One of the union guys gave him a friendly heads-up: "There's a contract out on you. Don't walk under any cranes."

When he heard *that*, he knew he'd made the right choice.

Barbara, Louis, and Stephanie did not take the news well. They loved Berwyn, and didn't understand why they had to once again uproot their lives and leave such an idyllic spot. The transition would prove difficult for all three of them. But Frank didn't let on that it was necessary to move for his own safety.

Midvale shut down two years later. Corruption and graft killed a company that was originally staffed by Civil War veterans. The parent company in Pittsburgh, where Joe Giacco worked, went belly-up in 1979. This was more of a surprise to Franklin, but he figured that the losses in the roll manufacturing department must have taken the entire company down.

"It was good you got out of there," I told him. "That place was busted out."

"Busted out?"

I explain that the mob, chronically thinking short-term, will take control of established businesses, extracting everything of value, borrowing on the company's credit, and, ultimately, dooming it to bankruptcy. "That's a bust out," I tell him. "And Philadelphia, at that time, was a hotbed of mob activity. The plant was near the railroad tracks, which means logistics. And all those union workers who can't be fired? The union bosses were either mobbed up, or had to at least deal with Little Nicky Scarfo, Angelo Bruno, and the crew. They were *Teamsters*, right?"

Frank looks at me in disbelief. He has good business sense, and the idea of destroying a successful company like this was inconceivable to him. But mobsters don't think like civilians. They think like criminals. They don't know how to build things. They only know how to destroy.

"It's good you got out of there," I tell him. "If you had blown the whistle, they would have had you killed for sure."

PART FOUR

WALLINGFORD

Frank in front of the mantle at his home
in Wallingford, ca. 1980.

22

MONTAGE

This is the fun part of the story.

In every biopic ever made about a famous musician, a singer like Johnny Cash or Elton John, or a rock band like The Doors or Queen, we come to the part where the artist has the Big Break. In the movie, this usually happens in a few minutes of screen time. The band is discovered by some portly, self-loathing record executive who will later screw them over, and the next thing you know, boom, everything comes up roses. We are treated to a montage: The creaky van is replaced by the private plane. The crappy apartment is swapped out for a fancy townhouse. The drummer buys a Rolls Royce with cash, just to stick it to the snooty car dealer. And so on.

These are the most dynamic scenes in the movie, because they signify not just success, but a jump in social standing, in economic class, in quality of life—all of it. I watch the NBA draft every year, partly for the same reason: these athletes, 19, 20, 21 years old, most from families of modest means, are selected by a professional basketball team and immediately become millionaires. That one life-changing moment is a culmination of talent, work ethic, desire, and, yes, luck.

Franklin St. John was born in a house without a toilet, in the farthest reaches of the Upper Peninsula. The odds were that he would wind up being a lumberjack, like his granddads, or a plowman, like his father. Not only did he manage to get an education and a good job as a metallurgical engineer, but he parlayed that knowledge, and his own skill set, into something even greater. Through talent, work ethic, desire, and, yes, luck, Frank became not just an engineer, but a wealthy one.

Luck: he didn't die in that L'Anse quicksand. Luck: he was given a medical deferment, and never had to serve in the military during the Vietnam War. Luck: he managed to escape Michigan without getting any of his perpetually ovulating girlfriends pregnant. Luck: he sat next to that stranger on an airplane, changing the trajectory of his life. Luck: he met Walter Jensen. Luck: the mobsters at Midvale didn't take him out.

What's interesting to me about Franklin's rise to riches is that he never set out to accumulate wealth, per se. He sees money as an indicator of success, but he's not greedy or rapacious, the way the Big Swinging Dicks of Wall Street infamy are. He's always been generous with his money—if more millionaires were wired like him, "trickle down" might have actually worked. And he's had fun with it. He's indulged himself. The nouveau riche get a bum rap, but only the newly wealthy, still marveling at their incredible good fortune, do joyful things like stuff ten grand in $20 bills and ship it certified mail to their sister in Michigan, or hire a local Italian to privately convey them around the sites in Rome, Florence, Milan, and Venice, or donate to the UConn Women's Basketball Team and take photos with Geno Auriemma and Diana Taurasi.

I remember once, 15 years ago or so, I was in his office when he unexpectedly received a check in the mail for $150,000.

"What do you do, when you get a check like that?" I asked out loud.

"First thing?" he said. "You do a little dance."

And then he did a little dance.

It's hard to begrudge a self-made millionaire his success when he's been so generous with his good fortune, and gotten so much enjoyment out of it. This is the sort of joy one finds in hip hop lyrics, when rappers boast of their rise from selling drugs on the corner to dropping gold records. Or in the song "Rosalita," by Bruce Springsteen, when he comes to take the titular lady out of her parents' house with big news:

> Someday we'll look back on this and it will all seem funny
> But now you're sad, your mama's mad,
> And your papa says he knows that I don't have any money,
> Whoa, your papa says he knows that I don't have any money,
> Whoa, so your daddy says he knows I don't have any money?
> Well, tell him this is his last chance to get his daughter in a fine romance,
> Because the record company, Rosie, just gave me a big advance!

When Frank moved back to Connecticut, tail between his legs, to take the job in the tiny gold company, working for Dr. Katz and with his old friend Walter Jensen, he thought he was lucky to have a job, after the near-fatal disaster in Nicetown.

Little did he know that he was about to have his "Rosalita" moment—and live out the American dream.

23

GOLDEN YEARS

THE NEW JOB COULD NOT HAVE BEEN more different from the one he left behind. Midvale was founded in the 19th century, an industry giant; a legend of business management had worked there; the company had hundreds of employees, enormous tanks, steel by the tonnage, and a customer base of blue-chip companies like GE.

Jennifer, by contrast, was a small family business, with just eight employees—Franklin was the ninth—and instead of being fantastically large, the scale was small. He went from working with 60-foot-high steel cylinders to ounces of gold alloys.

And unlike at Midvale, where he and Gilson were at odds, and the big cheese, Slocumb, was a crook, Dr. Katz was a good boss who treated him well. He taught him the ins and outs of the business, was generous with respect to salary and benefits, and seemed to genuinely enjoy his new employee's company. In his memoir, Frank describes him as "amazing."

Dr. Katz was five-two in his Florsheims, with a thinning head of hair and a paunch. Although he was a dentist by trade, his teeth were almost brown, on account of the long, malodorous cigars he was constantly chewing on. He was 68 years old when Frank started in January of 1974—old enough to be his father. In fact, Dr. Katz and Louis St. John were not only born in the same year—1905—but, coincidentally, would also die in the same year, 1979. Certainly there was a filial aspect to their relationship. But Katz had a son of his own: Gordon, a pathologist, who was Walter Jensen's neighbor, and plays an important role in our story. He also had three granddaughters, who were his pride and joy, and one of those enormous Cadillac Fleetwoods that were all the rage in the mid-70s, the floor of which was flecked by burn marks from stray cigar ashes. And he now had a successful business—the second one he'd started: an impressive accomplishment indeed.

During that first year at Jennifer, Frank and Dr. Katz struggled a bit to establish boundaries, especially concerning money. Here is a story that Frank has told me several times, meaning that for him, it signifies something larger than the story itself (which is rather mundane): One day, he needed to mail a letter and did not have the postage. So he knocked on Dr. Katz's door and asked if he could buy a stamp. At the time, stamps cost ten cents, and Dr. Katz told him to just take one. But Frank insisted on paying.

"That's ridiculous," Dr. Katz said. "It's a dime. Take the damn thing."

"It's like this: if you let me pay for the stamp, it saves me the trouble and expense of driving to the post office on my lunch break. Which I will be forced to do, if you don't let me pay for it."

So Frank got his stamp, and Dr. Katz, his dime.

"I could see," Frank wrote, many years later, "that he liked the way I handled the stamp situation."

Whether this minor incident made any sort of impression on Dr. Katz is debatable. What kind of maniac remembers buying a stamp in 1974? But in Frank's mind, he was setting a boundary. Yes, the stamp cost one thin dime, but it was the principle of the thing. He didn't want to feel like he was indebted to the man, or that he owed his boss anything.

Occasionally, the two of them would go to lunch, or to dinner after work. When they did, Dr. Katz let Frank drive his behemoth of an automobile, which Frank loved. "It handled beautifully, and it was so comfortable, it was almost like sitting in an easy chair in your living room." A year and a half after Frank started—a very profitable 18 months for Jennifer, as we shall see—Dr. Katz announced that he was buying a brand-new Cadillac, and that he would let Frank have his (not so) old one. The guy who insisted on paying for a ten-cent stamp decided it was okay to take the free Caddy. At that time, plenty of business executives had company cars. Why not him? (As he also points out, he'd *asked* for the stamp, which was something he needed; he neither asked for nor needed the car).

As it happened, the ethical dilemma was all for naught. A week or so later, the mechanic from Merriam Motors pulled up with the new Fleetwood, even longer and flashy than the old model. Then he got into the used car and drove it away, never to be seen again. Dr. Katz didn't say anything about it, so Frank didn't, either. But he was confused. He'd been promised a car, and didn't get one. Had the old man changed his mind? He continued to be confused, and more than a little resentful, until Walter told him what happened.

"It was Gordon. He told his father that a Fleetwood was too ostentatious for a man in your position."

"Ostentatious?"

"That was the word he used."

"What about the fact that his father promised me a car?"

"He didn't mention that."

Frank decided not to raise a stink about it. In fact, he didn't mention it at all. He didn't want either of the Katzs to think that it bothered him. But how could it not bother him? If Dr. Katz had guzzled one too many martinis when he promised him the used car, and then changed his mind, that's under-standable. A "luxury preowned" Cadillac wasn't cheap. But he should have had the decency to own up to it. Instead, he just waited cravenly for the unpleasantness to blow over.

Then there was the business with Barbara's dental work. All the cigarette smoking and coffee drinking and gun chewing and poor nutrition had wreaked havoc on her teeth. So Frank asked Dr. Katz, in his capacity as dentist, to have a look-see. Which he did. "She needs bridgework," he said, "and a few caps."

Dental work, then as now, doesn't come cheap. Once again, Dr. Katz wanted to be generous. "I can lend you whatever it costs to get her teeth fixed." Then, smiling through his own brown choppers, he said, "Just don't ask me for money." This was confusing, but Frank let it go. He had more than enough banked to cover the expense. So he contracted with his own dentist, and Barbara got her teeth fixed.

A few weeks later, Dr. Katz asked after Barbara, and wondered when Frank would need the loan.

"It's okay. I took care of it."

"You took care of it?"

"I borrowed the money from the bank," he lied.

"But I said I'd..."

"I know, but you didn't seem comfortable with it. It's okay, it's all fine."

"It's not fine," Dr. Katz said, reprimanding himself. "I should have just written you a check that day."

As Frank saw it—and I think he's right—Dr. Katz *wanted* to be generous, but didn't quite know how.

Despite the occasional weirdness, Frank did seem to like his mentor and vice versa. Certainly he learned about the gold business from him.

Gordon Katz, however, was another story.

24

METALLURGY

WHEN DR. KATZ STARTED JENNIFER, he outsourced the business of manufacturing the gold to an outside vendor. That worked swimmingly for some time, with both his company and the vendor enjoying outsized profits. But then the vendor got greedy, and decided, out of the blue and for no good reason, to double its rates. Like the dog in that Aesop fable who sees his own reflection in the lake, goes for the piece of meat that isn't really there, and loses the actual piece of meat in his jaws, the vendor wound up with nothing, when Dr. Katz wisely decided to set up his own manufacturing operation in-house, as I mentioned.

That's what Walter Jensen was originally hired to do: establish the gold manufacturing operation. And while he was a brilliant metallurgist, a genius in that field, he had no experience working with gold, and so was reluctant to take the offer.

"I'm not qualified," he told Frank one day, months earlier, over a diner lunch. "What happens when they figure out that I don't know what I'm doing?"

"Walter," Frank said. "Take the job."

"But I don't know the first thing about gold."

"Then you'll learn. You're a smart guy. You have all the textbooks. You'll figure it out. I mean, you're just *manufacturing* the gold, not transmuting it from iron or wood. This is metallurgy, not alchemy."

"I don't know."

"Walter," Frank said again. "Take. The. Fucking. Job."

Walter took the job, and as his friend had predicted, he figured it out.

When Frank first started at the company, in the winter of 1974, Walter taught him how to produce the gold alloys he'd developed. It was fascinating work, if you are a metallurgist; if you're an English major, it is, frankly, difficult to grasp. I'll include this description of the process from his memoirs, as a treat for the Michigan Tech metallurgical engineering alums who may be reading this:

> [Walter] had set up an induction coil and had graphite crucibles placed in the center of the coil. The coil was wired to the motor generator. The raw materials were then placed in the crucible and the MG was turned on and the melting process commenced. Borax was added to the molten metal in the crucible and the slag was poured off and what remained was the gold alloy. The purified alloy was then cast into an ingot in preparation for rolling. The weight of the ingot varied from 30 to 50 troy ounces. Remember at the steel mill the size of some of the ingots were over 100 tons. What a difference!

I have only ever heard of Borax from the brief period when my third grader was making "slime" out of Borax and Elmer's glue and some other magic ingredient I can't recall, and I have no idea what a "troy ounce" is, or how it may differ from the non-troy variety. The key takeaway from the metallurgical patois is the "MG." Without a motor generator, the refinement was impossible. And motor generators, as they would find out later, didn't come cheap.

For the first few months, Frank learned at his friend's side. He watched Walter—who, at six-three, was a giant of a man working with this very small material—as he rolled and slit the metal strips. Rather than wait for the process of slitting the alloys to finish, he'd devised a way of polishing them on a surface of highly polished chrome rolls, *as* he slit them. This saved the step of hand-polishing, and produced a nicer finish. Walter would then chop the strips into ingots, and stamp the company logo and the type of alloy on one side of the finished product.

Once he understood the basic processes, Frank began to work on developing other needed alloys. This must have been dull, even for him, because he glosses over it in his memoirs, where he has a habit of going into great detail about the science of this stuff. He soon realized that at Jennifer, unlike in his previous jobs, where he always put in long hours, there was not much actual work to be done. Walter could easily handle the metallurgical duties on his own.

And here we have another example of boredom bringing about inspiration. Franklin was, in his words, "not kept busy," and he is not the sort of person who is comfortable not being busy at work. So he took it upon himself to learn the other side of the business: the sales side.

In 1974, offices like this were still analog. Orders were taken by hand, with pen and paper. Sometimes customers would call up the toll-free number, responding to the ads Dr. Katz placed in the trade magazines. But usually they would mail in their order, with a check enclosed. Walter would stop by the post office on his way to work, and he or Dr. Katz would open the mail, envelope by envelope, using one of those snazzy letter-openers that my kids probably have no idea were once standard office equipment. Walter's wife, also named Barbara, was the bookkeeper. It was a family business. But Frank recognized that the business could grow. And he set about making that happen.

25

OUTBOUND SALES

MOST MODERN SALES TECHNIQUES can be traced back to Josiah Wedgwood, the eighteenth-century British potter turned entrepreneur turned abolitionist. Direct mail, money-back guarantees, free delivery, buy-one-get-one-free, illustrated catalogues—all of this stuff originated with Wedgwood, who died during George Washington's second term. (For all his myriad contributions to modern society, Wedgwood was the *second* most influential member of his family. His grandson was a botanist by the name of Charles Darwin.)

By 1974, marketing companies and advertising agencies had expanded on Wedgwood's original menu. The introduction of new media meant different avenues to boost sales. Companies ran ads on radio and television, or printed ads in newspapers and magazines. They sponsored events. All of that is *inbound* marketing—the idea is to lure the customer in, like the Venus flytrap to the fly. Outbound marketing is when the sales force actively reaches out to the customer. For decades, traveling salesmen roamed the country peddling their wares to captive housewives, most of whom had no interest in the encyclopedias, vacuum cleaners, or paint brushes that were on offer. The proliferation of the telephone in the fifties and sixties made outbound sales much easier. All the salesperson had to do was call a potential customer on the phone and give the pitch. Nine times out of ten, the salesman was hung up on. Nine times out of ten, the one person in ten who listened to the pitch turned it down politely. But the math worked out: The one percent of customers who ultimately bought the product more than made up for all the failures.

Jennifer hawked its wares to dentists. It had a core foundation of return customers, accumulated through Dr. Katz's many contacts in the industry, and wooed new customers with advertisements in various dental trade magazines. There were a lot of customers, certainly, but only a tiny fraction of the total number of dentists in the country and beyond. So Franklin did what Josiah Wedgwood could have only dreamed of: he picked up the phone and began cold-calling dentists.

And what he pitched them was nothing short of brilliant. It was a product he called "J-24." The "J" stood for "Jennifer." The "24" was the number of karats in the product. Basically, he was offering pure gold, but masquerading it as a dental alloy—a tax deductible business expense. Enterprising dentists could buy "J-24," write it off on their taxes, and then do with it whatever they wanted. Most of the "J-24" went right from the Jennifer vault to the dentists' safe deposit boxes, where it would remain.

In the seventies, there were wild fluctuations in the price of gold. In 1970, it was $39 an ounce. Four years later, an ounce cost $184. A dentist who bought $50,000 of "J-24" in 1975 or '76 would be sitting on over 200 grand, if he unloaded it at the peak of the market in 1980.

Frank sold "J-24" by the kilo, for eight bucks an ounce above market price. There are 32.15 troy ounces per kilo, so for every kilo sold, Jennifer made $257 in pure profit. In effect, the dentists were paying an eight dollar surcharge to be able to write the purchase off against their income. But the dentists who bought the "J-24" would also buy Jennifer's other products.

Frank's outbound sales pitch succeeded beyond his wildest dreams. The operation was so profitable that the company hired a full-time salesman just to work the phones—Brian

LaTouche, a friend of Franklin's from his days selling wigs, one of his many unusual sidelines.

Dr. Katz enjoyed boasting about the company's success to his cronies in Florida, where he whiled away the winter months. He would call up the office just before closing time for a report on the day's activities. This was done more for him to regale his crew than for actual business purposes, so Frank would indulge him, spinning a good yarn. But the bottom line didn't lie. Jennifer was a huge success. And Frank was a big reason why.

To his credit, Dr. Katz recognized who was responsible for the windfall. And despite withholding used Cadillacs, he was generous in compensation. After the first year, he gave Frank a thousand dollar bonus, and bumped up his salary to $23,000 from $20,000. In April of 1975, not quite a year and a half into his career with the company, Frank was promoted to Executive Vice President, given a $5,000 increase in salary, and a gas credit card. By the time Dr. Katz went to Florida from the winter of '75, Frank was running the day-to-day operations of the company. He was even in charge of his friend Walter Jensen! He was given yet another $5,000 raise, as well as a $2,500 bonus. That doesn't sound like much, but if we adjust for inflation, we see he was making almost $200k a year in today's dollars.

Frank was on top of the world. He was running a great, successful company. He was driving a new Cadillac of his own. He was in possession of a gas card. He had a lovely Cape Cod house on a babbling stream in Wallingford, across from an apple orchard.

And then, as he put it, "the roof fell in on me." Gordon Katz—Leon's son; the one who told his father that a used Cadillac Fleetwood with cigar burns on the carpet was too ostentatious for a man in Frank's position—decided he was sick of being a pathologist. He wanted to join the family business.

And he was bringing both his wife and his best friend, Marty Shulmann, with him.

The writing was on the wall. It was time for Frank to take action.

26

MANSION ROAD

THE WALLINGFORD HOUSE WAS ON MANSION ROAD, which would, a decade and a half later, become something of a joke among Louis, Stephanie, and their friends. "*Of course* Dr. St. John the millionaire lives on *Mansion* Road." Despite the fancy moniker, that thoroughfare runs through apple orchards, farmland, and sturdy split-levels and raised ranches. It's unclear if the name derives from the road leading *to* a mansion, or from the one creaky old house that, when it was built right after the Civil War, may have qualified as a mansion at the time the street was christened. By the time the St. John family moved back to Connecticut, however, "Mansion Road" was an unequivocal misnomer.

Not that the environs weren't lovely, in that Middle-Atlantic-heading-to-New-England sort of way. Their house was a Cape Cod, all dormer windows and sloped ceilings, with three bedrooms, a kitchen (where Barbara spent most of her time), two-and-a-half bathrooms—that is, three more toilets than Franklin had in his house growing up—and a breezeway leading from the house to the detached garage.

They were constantly putting additions on the house. But when I first visited in 2000, the breezeway still contained the wooden paneling peculiar to TV rooms of the 1970s, an enormous console television, and a La-Z-Boy recliner where Frank sat huddled under blankets because there was no heater out there: a millionaire in repose.

Wallingford is a sprawling town of some 45,000 people—40 square miles of land on either side of the Quinnipiac River. That vast expanse contains multitudes. There is a state road lined with strip malls and box stores, indistinguishable from any other big town's main drag in the Northeast. There are factories, manufacturing plants, industrial centers. There is a lovely state park, where the day after Christmas a few years ago my brother-in-law made us all climb the icy trail to the top of the mountain. There is a huge postal hub, made famous in the days after 9/11, when anthrax was discovered there. And there are Quinnipiac University, renowned for its polling, and Choate-Rosemary Hall, one of the most exclusive boarding schools in the country, which both Lou and Stephanie would later attend.

Founded in 1667, Wallingford has the dubious distinction of being the site of the last witchcraft trial in New England. An alleged witch named Winifred Benham was thrice accused—and, thankfully, thrice acquitted—of being in league with the devil. Because it's so spread out, and so old, Wallingford feels more like a quilt than a cohesive place—at least to me. I have been visiting for 20 years and I still can't quite figure out the geography; even my wife, who grew up there, will sometimes make a wrong turns. Perhaps this is the ghost of Winifred Benham, haunting us.

Lou was old enough to have made some good friends in Berwyn, whom he was reluctant to leave behind. He didn't know any kids in the new neighborhood, and the first summer in Wallingford, he was restless and bored. As a boy, he liked to play sports. He was forever throwing around a whiffle ball or a football, or shooting baskets. And he was competitive about it. He played to win. With no one else to play with, he took the desperate step of recruiting his kid sister, who was then five, into his games. He taught her how to throw a ball, how to swing a bat, how to run bases. This must have been frustrating—Stephanie was five full years younger, and a girl, and not much interested in competitive sports—but she enjoyed the attention, and did her level best to keep up. While it was not obvious in the moment, he did a good job training her. Stephanie can still throw a ball with surprising velocity, catch a football, and make decent contact when she swings a bat.

A story Franklin loves to tell involves Stephanie's curious combination of being naturally athletic and not remotely competitive. She played softball in Little League. She was talented, but wasn't particularly jazzed about it. Up at bat, she drilled a ball to the gap between third and short. She tossed aside the bat and sprinted towards first base. But instead of running *through* the base, as she'd been taught to do by Louis, and her father, and the softball coach, she let up, so that she would stop on the base. The result was that the throw beat her to first, and she was called out. "She should have kept running!" Franklin says, laughing.

I can't tell you how many times I've heard this rather lame story—a disproportionate amount relative to its inherent interest. How many other young kids don't run through first base? All of them, probably. But something in that little vignette informs Frank's understanding of his daughter—who badly wanted to fit in with her sporty, competitive father and brother, but didn't quite have it in her. (For her part, Stephanie insists that she knew to run through the base, and always had).

What none of them seemed to understand was that Stephanie was the glue of that family. The workaholic father, logging long hours at his new job, taking side gigs on the weekend, and pursuing an advanced degree. A brother five years older, scarred by being abandoned for a month when he was a baby, rebellious by nature, increasingly angry at his increasingly detached parents. And a mother always on the verge of a psychotic break. Even as a young girl, my wife intuitively recognized the difficult personalities at work, and sought to be the bridge among all of them. It must have been emotionally exhausting—in Berwyn, at least, she could steal away in the dining room of Mudsy and Harriet. In Wallingford, there was nowhere to hide.

Barbara, too, did not take to her new home. Now she was closer to her family, which, in her case, was never a good thing. It was after the return to Connecticut, when Stephanie was five, that Barbara once again was admitted to the mental hospital. This was during the first year at Jennifer, when Frank was working six days a week, *and* taking classes at night. The kids were too much for Barbara to handle. Lack of adequate supervision was a constant for Stephanie and Lou.

But Frank was also making a lot of money—much more than he had before—and money can solve a lot of problems. Every year, they would go down the shore on summer vacation, to Ocean City, New Jersey. This tradition started when they still lived in Pennsylvania—Ocean City is toward the southern end of the Jersey shore, closer to Philadelphia than New York. Back then, they could only afford a small house far away from the beach and the boardwalk. With each successive year, as Frank made more and more money, the house they rented got bigger, nicer, and closer to the prime beachfront locations. Louis and Stephanie both still love that town, and Ocean City was Barbara's favorite place on earth. On random, gloomy March mornings, she would smile at them and say, "Just think, kids—Ocean City!"

Years later, after she passed on New Year's Day 2003, Stephanie and I disposed of her ashes in Ocean City. It was after midnight, and we were both extremely drunk. We put Barbara's remains in a plastic bucket, of the kind children use to make sandcastles, and staggered to the beach. With a plastic shovel, we dug a hole on the wet part of the sand, and transferred the ashes from the bucket to the hole. Then the surf came and took her away.

Even in the dim moonlight, we could see that the remains were lighter in color than the sand. As the waves came in and out, and the ashes dispersed, it looked like the white silhouette of a head and extended arms—or maybe wings.

It looked like the outline of an angel.

27

420 TROY OUNCES

THERE WERE TWO FACTORS that informed the decision by Franklin St. John and Walter Jensen to leave Jennifer and start their own company. First was the move by Dr. Katz to bring his son, Gordon, into the business. Gordon had been Walter's neighbor, and it was Gordon who recruited him to the company in the first place; we can safely assume that the two men were friendly, if not friends.

But Frank and Gordon were oil and water. To Frank, the son joining a company founded by the aging father could only mean that one day, he would be working for, and not with, Gordon Katz. And that was something he would never do. That Gordon was bringing in his wife—who Frank wound up training—and his best friend Marty Shulmann was a sign that he wanted his own people there, that Frank did have his full trust. There was also the religious aspect. Marty was the president of the local synagogue. Dr. Katz was Jewish, as were his son and daughter-in-law. This wasn't anti-Semitism—Frank has never been a prejudiced person—as much as self-preservation. To Frank, this was another excuse for them to get rid of him. After all, he was a practicing Catholic with the least Jewish surname possible.

The second factor is that Jennifer appeared to be cheating Walter Jensen out of his dividends. When he joined the company as the head metallurgist—arguably the most critical employee—Walter was given a 25 percent stake in the company, as we have discussed. These were generous terms, and he more than lived up to them.

One winter day—while Dr. Katz was down in Florida, and right before Gordon began working there—Walter showed off his dividend check.

"Check this out," he said, pushing the check across the table. "Eleven large. Pretty sweet, huh?" And indeed, the check was for a whopping $11,250.

"Walter," Frank said, "don't you have a 25 percent stake?"

"Yeah."

"Then you have a problem."

"A problem? With an eleven thousand dollar check?"

"Look: the full dividend is for $75,000."

"Right."

"Divide eleven and a quarter by 75."

Walter did the math. Then his face turned beet red. "Why, that no good…"

The dividend check meant Walter had a *15* percent stake in Jennifer, not the 25 he'd been promised. In practical terms—this will be important later—only 15 percent of the gold scrap in the company vault belonged to Walter. There was a ten percent discrepancy. He was being screwed.

In a series of meetings held far away from the Jennifer offices, and long after work hours, Frank and Walter decided to start up their own business—in direct competition with the Katzs. (In those days, I guess, employees didn't have to sign non-compete contracts.) Frank knew how to make the alloys, and certainly could move product. Walter knew how to set up shop, as he'd done the same for Jennifer a few years prior. And they'd been friends for years, so there was enormous trust. It was a perfect marriage.

They began to hatch the plan. The biggest obstacle was the motor generator, an exorbitantly expensive piece of machinery critical to the operations. They were able to find one to lease, but it would take until April 1, 1976 for delivery. In the meantime, they would acquire the rest of the equipment second-hand, and iron out the wrinkles on the fly.

The key, during this period, was keeping what they were doing a secret from Gordon Katz.

The solution was sneaky brilliant and devious as hell. The two friends pretended to be at odds, and would be openly hostile to each other when they were in the office. Walter was so convincing that it made Frank suspect that maybe he really *was* mad at him. In one instance, when some or other mistake was made, Walter snapped, "That lousy Frenchman screwed it all up!" This led to Gordon Katz reprimanding him for using an ethnic slur—an honorable move, in my opinion.

In the spring of '76, Gordon was made president of Jennifer. He was now everyone's direct supervisor. The first item on the agenda was to make nice with his highest-earning employee. So he summoned Frank into his office. "I know you don't like me," he said, in what was the preamble to a carefully crafted speech. But he never finished the prepared remarks, because Frank cut him off:

"That's right, Gordon. I don't."

This belligerent response took the mild-mannered Gordon by surprise. He foundered for a minute, then regained his footing. "Even though there's no love lost between us, we can still work together."

"Oh, of *course*," Frank said.

But the die had already been cast. Now it was a matter of extricating themselves from Jennifer, financing the start-up company—and making sure Walter got the full 25 percent of what was owed him.

FRANK SPENT the next two months getting his finances in order. He sold a piece of property he owned in Newtown, Connecticut for $15,000. He obtained another $15,000 when he took out a second mortgage on the Wallingford house.

"I offered to mortgage my wife and children," he joked, "but the bank said no."

Walter's capital was tied up in Jennifer. By rights, 25 percent of the scrap gold in the company's vault belonged to him. The problem was, there was never an inventory taken of the holdings. It was an arduous, unnecessary process, so they never bothered. Frank knew how to estimate the value of scrap; Dr. Katz had dutifully showed him how. He determined that there was $200,000 worth in the vault, meaning $50,000 worth was Walter's.

To extract the requisite amount, they needed to produce about 420 troy ounces of gold from the scrap. So Walter set about systematically refining the scrap—on weekends and at night, while no one else was around. It took a few weeks, but he managed to accumulate 420 troy ounces, *and* remove it from the premises, without being discovered. Only after his own share was safely out of the Jennifer vault did he propose to Gordon that they refine the scrap in the vault, which he then set about doing.

"Was this outright dishonest, or was this justified?" Frank reflects in this memoir. "Like I said before, it's always easy to justify things that benefit you. The only thing I know for sure is that, if Walter had ever asked for his portion of the scrap, he would never have gotten it."

The 420 troy ounces of gold salvaged from Walter Jensen's portion of the scrap in the vault ultimately wound up being used in alloys made by the new company: Jensen Industries Inc. Although Frank owned fully half the company, he wanted to keep his extremely Christian name off it, so as not to turn off Jewish dentists, of whom there was a significant number.

Walter gave notice in March of 1976. So successfully did he and Frank pretend to hate each other that no one at Jennifer even asked Frank how he felt about the situation. The two of them rented out a three-car garage, which they stocked with the machinery they would need to hit the ground running. Once the motor generator arrived that April, they would be good to go.

A week or two after Walter's departure, Dr. Katz took Frank out to dinner. After a few drinks, the older man began to read him the riot act: "I don't understand why you and Gordon can't get along. You don't have to be best friends, but you're not even trying!"

Frank could tell that this was eating at him: His son and his favorite employee, to whom he was something of a father figure, were at war. So he decided to bring down the hammer. "Let me stop you right there, Dr. Katz. I'm leaving Jennifer."

"What?"

"Let this be my two weeks' notice."

Dr. Katz looked crestfallen. He took a sip of his martini. He reflected on this unexpected and undesired turn of events for a moment. Finally, he asked, "If I hadn't brought Gordon into the business, would you be quitting?"

"Probably not," Frank replied. "But I'll tell you this: if Gordon were my son, I'd have done the same thing."

Absolved, Dr. Katz nodded. "What are you going to do?"

"Do? Oh, I'm going back to the old job in Philadelphia."

The next day, Frank arrived at the office a few minutes late. Dr. Katz, Gordon, and the management team told him he was to leave the premises immediately, and gave him a check for the two weeks' pay. And that was the end of his employment.

His time at Jennifer had been short, fruitful, and mostly enjoyable, notwithstanding his inability to coexist with the boss's son. What happened next was the biggest risk of his life. But as UConn Women's Basketball Coach Geno Auriemma once said: If you don't take risks, you never win big.

28

FAILURE TO LAUNCH

IF THE WAIT FOR THE MOTOR GENERATOR was excruciatingly long, the interval between Frank walking out the door and the new company being fully operational happened at warp speed. There was Frank and Walter Jensen. There was Walter's wife, Barbara, who did the books. Frank's friend Brian LaTouche, another Jennifer employee, defected and joined the team, bringing with him his girlfriend, Susan Voscheck, who became the office manager. Rounding out the maiden staff was Gene Zurillo, who ran a business selling scrap gold from dentists to Jennifer; after getting wind of the new concern, he was hired as a commission salesman.

The name of the new company was Jensen Industries. As I mentioned, Franklin wanted his surname off it, because of the religious connotations. "You couldn't have a more Christian name than St. John," he said, "and a large percentage of the dentists in the country were Jewish. Now, Jensen is a very neutral Danish name. In fact, during World War II, the Danes refused to give over their Jewish population to the Nazis." But that wasn't the only reason. "I thought I would be able to manage the employees better," he reasoned, "if they thought I was an employee and not an owner."

Any mystery about the identity of the company's ownership structure dissipated within days of the company officially opening its doors, however. On Friday of that first week, Frank went home for lunch. He came back to find Gene Zurillo in the doorway of the office, jumping up and down and waving a piece of paper back and forth like he was doing semaphore.

"You gotta see this, Frank. It's unbelievable."

"What is it?"

"It's unbelievable. Un-be-*liev*-able."

The paper was an injunction, signed by the local judge. The new company was being sued by Jennifer, for theft of business and a laundry list of other alleged malfeasances. Per the injunction, they were not to solicit business from any of Jennifer's customers.

It's a good thing Frank had already eaten his lunch, because he lost his appetite. He thought of the land he sold in Newtown, the second mortgage, the gold scrap Walter had taken out of the vault. There was a ton of money invested in the new company. There were employees, laboratory space, office space. There was a lease on a piece of heavy machinery. This was a nightmare.

As it happened, Barbara Jensen's sister's husband's father—the father of the husband of the sister of the wife of Walter Jensen, in other words—was a prominent New Haven attorney named N. Randall Basset. (You can tell he was prominent because of that first initial before the name). Jensen Industries retained Basset and a trial lawyer, James O'Shea, who prepared their defense.

This was not like a trial in Kafka or *Bleak House* that continues interminably. It seems that the fancy attorney managed to fast-track the case. Two weeks after Gene Zurillo waved the paper—a fortnight of no little anxiety for Frank and Walter—the decision came down.

There was good news and bad news. The bad news was, Frank and Walter lost. The good news was, the injunction didn't bother their business in the least. The result of the ruling was that the Jensen sales team could not call any Jennifer customers directly. But nothing prevented them from going through the phone book and cold-calling dentists in various cities—and if some of them turned out to be Jennifer customers, oh well, so be it. So that's what they did. Brian LaTouche and Gene Zurillo went through phonebooks, dialing up every dentist they could find. They wound up with a lot of Jennifer customers—and some new ones, too.

Not only that, but when the judge initially forced them to not call any dentists, for fear of hitting upon a Jennifer customer, the sales staff instead tried their luck with dental *laboratories*. That provided a whole new revenue stream. One of their biggest customers, in fact, was a consortium of dental labs in Japan.

Since this is the last time Frank's former bosses figure in the story, I should add that despite Jensen Industries poaching some of their business, things didn't end badly for Leon and Gordon Katz. On the contrary, Jennifer continued to be extraordinarily profitable. Far from ruining the family business, as Frank predicted he would, Gordon Katz proved a shark. At one point, the former pathologist took the company public. The IPO stood at $5 a share, which climbed up to $7. Then the price plummeted. When it hit a buck a share, Gordon Katz bought back all of the outstanding stock. In that deal alone, he walked away with millions of dollars.

Franklin and Walter wound up succeeding beyond their wildest dreams in business for themselves, as we shall soon see. My father-in-law did not have an ownership stake in Jennifer, and likely never would have. Had they stayed with the Katzs, however, he wouldn't have gone belly-up.

Either of the paths he could have chosen were paved with gold.

29

BIG TIME

THERE WAS MORE TO FRANK'S SUCCESS than cold-calling dentists. Sales is a tough job, and unappealing if you're not wired the right way, but even so, there are a hundred thousand salesmen who could have worked the phones like he did at Jennifer. Success requires talent, work ethic, desire, and more than a little luck. But to really hit the big time, you also need a sprinkle of that magical fairy dust that is genius.

Ultimately, Jensen Industries made its fortune not because of talent, hard work, or luck—although the company enjoyed all of those things—but through genius. Frank and Walter developed a product of their own—one that no one else could have come up with. The product was called "Unitbond." It was an alloy of nickel, chromium, and beryllium that could bond with porcelain: for dentists, a cheap substitute for gold. And it would make the two entrepreneurs rich.

The seeds of the idea were all in place. Frank started the new company with the secret formula already percolating in his metallurgist's brain. All that was left to do was run tests and make sure that the alloy would, in fact, bond to porcelain. To do this would require both time and money.

The usual way to manufacture an alloy like this was to melt the metals in a vacuum, as they used to do at Jennifer. But Jensen Industries did not have a vacuum melting system lying around the three-car garage. And to procure one would cost 80 grand, minimum. Which they did not have. What to do?

Melting a nickel-chromium alloy in air would cause oxidation, and the oxidized alloy, they knew, would *not* bond to porcelain. The trick was to devise an alternative method of manufacturing the alloy that *didn't* require the purchase of $80,000 worth of new equipment.

"Well," Walter said, "we could always melt it in a reducing atmosphere."

Frank thought about this. "Yes," he said. "That would work, I think. At least in theory. In practice, though?"

"I know. It's difficult."

"Difficult but not impossible."

"No," Walter said. "Not impossible." And Frank could see the proverbial wheels turning in his friend's big brain. Jensen's mind was like a roulette wheel. It would keep spinning around until it landed on the winning solution.

It took about six weeks, but Walter solved the problem. The process involved melting the alloy elements using a blanket of hydrogen. Which was dangerous. I'm no chemist, but even I know that hydrogen, when disturbed, can do things like obliterate whole cities. The last thing Walter wanted to do was blow the lab, or half of Wallingford, to smithereens.

I'll let Frank explain this, because I may as well be transcribing it from Aramaic:

What the process consisted of was the use of two free-standing silica crucibles, one inverted on top of the other. A two-inch round hole was cut out where the two crucibles contacted each other, and a tube was inserted into the hole. The hydrogen would flow into the cavity formed by the crucibles. The next problem was the proper procedure for melting the raw ingredients. We learned that the proper layering of the raw ingredients in the crucible was critical. Not to go into this more deeply, but it was necessary that the chromium be put on the bottom, followed by the Ni-Be and Al, and finally the pure Ni.

The process was so revolutionary that they could have applied for a patent. But they didn't do so. A patent would just show their competitors the blueprint for how to do it. And Jensen Industries didn't have the resources necessary to make potential copycats stop.

Unitbond was the pure collaboration of the two company founders. Frank came up with the formula for the alloy. Walter figured out how to manufacture it on the cheap. One would not have succeeded without the other. It was an equal partnership: a bond. An alloy.

And boy, did it pay off.

It's not difficult to understand why. At the time, Jensen Industries was selling gold alloys for between $120 and $200 an ounce. Gold alloys, as I have mentioned, are useful in dentistry because gold is one of few metals that bonds with teeth.

Unitbond did the same thing. It was, literally, as good as gold. But it was much, much cheaper. Here is the wholesale pricing structure for the new product when it was launched in 1976:

- 1 ounce @ $16.95
- 3 ounces @ $14.95/oz.
- 10 ounces @ $13.95/oz.
- 100 ounces @ $10.95/oz.
- 1,000 ounces @ $6.95/oz

It addition to being vastly less expensive, Unitbond matched the color of the teeth better. And it was not as dense as the gold alloys, so dental labs could make it last longer than the same amount of a gold alloy. Basically, it was a dream come true for the dentists.

Oh, and the best part? It cost a mere 40 cents an ounce to manufacture. So a lab that purchased 100 ounces of Unitbond would make the company $1055 in profit—the $1,095 sale price less the $40 manufacturing cost. Frank hired more salesmen, promoted Gene Zurillo to be their manager, and set up an attractive commission schedule of a buck an ounce. Not that customers were buying a *single* ounce of the stuff. Frank says he can't recall one instance of that happening. Orders were always for many ounces.

And there were a lot of orders. I mean, an absolute shit-ton.

After just two months in business, Jensen Industries was already turning a profit. It was a harbinger of good things to come. The company, a sub-chapter S Corporation, officially opened its doors on April 1, 1976. That July, Frank and Walter both began drawing $1,000 a month. In September, that increased to $1,500 a month each. They each took a grand as a year-end bonus, and that December, increased the draw to $2,500 each. By the end of the following year, they were each drawing $10,000 a month. In 1978, it was $20,000. The amount gradually increased to a whopping $75,000 per month.

As if that wasn't enough, this windfall coincided with Ronald Reagan reducing the top marginal tax rate, which had been over 90 for most of the 1950s, from 70 to 50 percent, and then, in his second term, to a mere 28 percent. Frank told me that in his best years, that meant anywhere from 250 to 300 grand went to him instead of Uncle Sam.

Not that Uncle Sam didn't try to take its cut from Jensen Industries. A few years into the business, during a cold spell in March, the IRS dispatched an auditor to check the company's books. He was cocky, Frank recalled—a real ballbuster. He was exactly the sort of guy my father-in-law loves nothing more than to troll.

"I need to see the documentation for your company cars."

"I'm not sure what you mean," Frank said.

"As you're no doubt aware, some of the yearly mileage on company cars is allocated for personal use. I'm going to take a look-see at those numbers."

"Well," Frank said, "I'm sorry to say that we can't provide that for you."

The T-man licked his chops. "Oh no?"

"We don't have any company cars."

Deflated, the auditor actually stammered in disbelief.

"Yeah. The BMW in the parking lot is my personal ride."

"Well, I'm still going to do an audit. I'll be back first thing in the morning. You'll have to provide me some office space to use, while I go through the books."

"Whatever you say."

At the time, Jensen Industries was leasing space next to cold storage vaults used to store furs. Frank's office was adjacent to those vaults, where it could get quite cold. That night, before going home, he unplugged the electric heater and hid it in a utility closet. By the time the auditor arrived the next morning, the office was an icebox. You could almost see your breath.

"You can take my office," Frank said, feigning gallantry.

"A bit cold in here, no?"

"Is it? I'm from the Upper Peninsula of Michigan. The cold doesn't bother me. It reminds me of home."

The guy lasted an hour and a half, and they passed the audit without any problems.

As I SAID, this is the fun part of the story. This was when Frank began to endow the metallurgical engineering department at Michigan Tech. (I don't know how much he donated, but eventually they gave him an honorary doctorate, which tend to be much more expensive than the non-honorary variety.) This is when he stuffed ten grand in a shoebox and mailed it to his sister Jeanie back in Michigan. This is when he bought himself a new car every other year, always a fast model, and tossed his many speeding tickets into the glovebox. This is when he rented fancy beach houses and sent his kids (and, in one instance involving a friend of Louis's whose father suddenly and unexpectedly died, other kids) to swanky boarding schools.

But for all his success in his professional life, his home life was falling apart.

30

I LEFT MY HEART IN SAN FRANCISCO

MONEY SOLVED A LOT OF PROBLEMS. Certainly Franklin's new-found wealth meant he could afford whatever prescription drugs or psychiatric care Barbara might require. But you can't buy off mental illness.

Pills worked if she took them. Her delusions went away. She stopped believing spirits were trying to communicate with her through the patterns of license plates on the Merritt Parkway. But when she took them, she didn't feel like herself. She was tired, fuzzy, a little bit out of it—like a dimmer switch had been deployed on her brain. So she would stop taking her pills, and for a brief shining moment, she'd feel spectacular. Suddenly she was herself again. Suddenly everything was clear and in sharper focus and made sense. And then the bad feelings would come back, and the license plate cipher, and the delusions.

Frank was better than most at being able to compartmentalize—to keep work matters confined to the office, libidinal matters confined to the bedroom, family matters confined to the kitchen table. And there were never issues in the office, as we have seen, or, somehow, the bedroom. He has told me on numerous occasions that he and Barbara—how shall I phrase this?—enjoyed each other's company every single day that they were together—even at the end, when their marriage was unravelling. I'm sure there is some exaggeration there, but even so, their sex life, as far as he was concerned, was just fine.

But the family stuff: that was the nest of thorns. Barbara wasn't happy. She wasn't taking her meds. She was inventing affairs with Frank's co-workers—Gene Zurillo, this time. She was withdrawing. He was at work a lot, or else taking night courses, and rarely came home except to sleep, eat, or make love. So there was not a lot of parenting going on at Mansion Road. Louis was a rebellious teenager, who was eventually shipped off to Choate. But Stephanie was in sixth grade when her parents got divorced. Too often, she was forced to fend for herself.

The straw that broke the back of this particular camel was a dollop of syrup that my wife, who was ten years old, spilled on her new pink sweater. The three of them—Frank, Barbara, and Stephanie—were planning to leave later that day for a trip to San Francisco, a short and much-needed getaway.

"There's a stain on your sweater," Frank noted. "You should get changed before we go."

"All my clothes are packed," Stephanie said.

This sent him into a fury. "Barbara! What do you do with all the money I give you to buy the kids clothes?"

Stephanie didn't say she didn't *have* clothes, just that the clothes she had were all packed. No matter. This escalated into a screaming fight, culminating in Barbara screaming, "That's it! I've had it! I want a divorce!" It was during the row that she made a point to tell him that the new love of her life, Gene Zurillo, his sales manager, would come to her rescue.

The trip to San Francisco never happened. In fact, Frank made his disappointed and probably terrified daughter accompany him to the travel agency, to refund the tickets.

The next day, Barbara recanted. Her mood cleared. She was suddenly lucid. Now she didn't want a divorce. But Frank played off her emotions, allowing her to believe he was taking her back, while working with an attorney and preparing the paperwork. He loved Barbara, I do believe that, but he was simply not equipped to handle her mental illness. I don't know that anyone could have been.

Frank was generous in the settlement. He paid her a handsome alimony. He let her stay in the Mansion Road house with the kids, relocating himself to a sad raised ranch in North Haven that, as Stephanie recalls, "screamed 'temporary.'"

This was a difficult, confusing time for my wife. When I asked her about it, she gave me the details, and then was noticeably gloomy and morose after. These were not fond memories.

Now Stephanie was in the house with a mother who, while a loving person, was abjectly unfit. Once, when she was 11 years old, Barbara took her to a Singles Night event at a local bar. Stephanie had developed early, so she looked older than she was, but even so: a bar?

"I remember I was there with my mom, and I was dressed up so I looked older, and this man walks up to me…"

And in my mind, I'm assuming the man is some lecherous pervert, but no. He wasn't coming over to hit on her, but to save her. "How old are you?" She told him. "You shouldn't be here. This is a place for grown-ups." And to Barbara: "What are you doing, taking an 11-year-old to a bar? What's wrong with you?"

Barbara did not have malicious intentions. She just didn't understand that this was inappropriate. She brought Stephanie for the simple reason that she didn't want to go to Singles Night all by herself—and she had no one else to bring.

"It was one of the many times that I learned from the reactions of *other* people—strangers—that the way my mother was behaving was not normal," Stephanie recalled.

This happened over 40 years ago. Barbara has been dead for 20 years. Even so, that story strikes me as horribly, horribly sad. I feel bad for my wife. I feel bad for Barbara. It's just awful all around.

31

TALES OF A METALLURGIST

JENSEN INDUSTRIES SPECIALIZES in the manufacture of dental alloys. At first blush, that sounds pretty dull. But to make dental alloys, you have to have the requisite raw materials. Some of those raw materials were precious metals: gold, silver, palladium. This meant that the company was constantly having to spend huge sums of money just to acquire the raw materials. Not only that, but the price of precious metals was constantly in flux. In the late seventies and eighties, the price of gold was cuckoo. So Frank had to not only acquire the stuff—which could be dangerous, as it sometimes involved trips to the less seemly boroughs of New York City—but also make sure there was enough cash or credit to purchase it—and not be left holding the hot potato if the gold price collapsed.

Who knew there was such volatility in tooth reconstruction?

The first of the problems involved a credit crunch. Jensen Industries did not exist in March of 1976. By the end of the year, it was doing a fantastic amount of business. There was a tremendous quantity of cash coming in, but also a tremendous quantity going out, because of the urgent need for the expensive raw materials. In the early years—long before logistics companies like UPS and FEDEX offered overnight delivery—the company literally could not afford to wait for the post office to deliver the precious metals. So Frank would go to the city to fetch the stuff.

In the seventies, New York City was at its nadir. This was the era where the subway trains were full of graffiti, when crime was rampant, when the city was teetering on the verge of bankruptcy, and when the famous headline ran in the *Daily News*: FORD TO CITY: DROP DEAD.

Frank would take the Amtrak from New Haven to Penn Station. From there, he'd have to hit two stops: Republic Bank, for the gold, and Leytess Metals, for the palladium. And the quickest way between them was on the subway, which, as mentioned, was kind of sketchy. He bought a ladies' pocketbook, with a cheesy floral print. He didn't shave. He wore an old shirt. He didn't shower. And, in case his fellow passengers didn't get the message, he bought a copy of *Playboy* and left the centerfold opened in his lap. He looked like a pervy bum. He looked nothing at all like a guy who had thousands of dollars' worth of precious metals in his terrible handbag. (The *Playboy* was probably not necessary, but I'm sure this was merely a convenient excuse to justify checking out Miss November in all her airbrushed glory).

The real problem was the credit crunch. At the end of the day, it was a math problem: ultimately, the company spent much, much less than it brought in, but to get the ball rolling required an enormous amount of front-end capital. Jensen's assets were tied up in gold, other precious metals, and accounts receivable. And because the company was new, banks, being generally run by conservative functionaries with zero imagination, were not keen on ponying up the needed cash.

The company did its banking with North Haven National Bank, a small, local institution down the road from Frank's house in Wallingford. After meeting with the managers, they were given a $50,000 credit line, putting their homes up as collateral. Two months later, the cash was gone—used to buy the raw materials to service their many customers. So they went back to the bank, which, with great reluctance, released another $45,000, which was North Haven National's lending limit. Two months later, same problem.

It looked like their problems would be solved organically, when North Haven National was gobbled up by The Second New Haven Bank. The larger lender had a limit of $250,000, which was closer to what Jensen needed. And they were quickly approved for the full limit.

Until, suddenly, they weren't. Instead of extending their credit, the bank called in the loan. Frank called and hollered at them, incensed that they didn't honor their commitment, but to no avail. Apparently the bank had a new manager who was a bit of a tight-ass.

"This is crazy," Walter complained. "I mean, we may be forced out of business because we're doing *too* well."

If they couldn't find a bank to extend more credit, that's exactly what would happen—all their hard work would be for naught.

"Don't worry," Frank told his friend. "I'm not worried."

But this was not true. He was extremely worried. Worse, he knew that, as the "outside man" of the operation, the onus was on him to save the day. So he put together a formal business plan, polished up his resume, and went to the banks, hat in hand.

"I don't remember how many turned us down," he said. "But it was a lot."

But just as it only takes one buyer to sell a house, so it only takes one bank to approve your credit. Frank finally found that one banker: Len Suzio, of American National Bank. Suzio was a young hot-shot type, who liked what he saw. He arranged for Bank of Boston to be the correspondent bank, and saw to it that Jensen Industries got a million-dollar line of credit, using inventory (gold!) and receivables as collateral.

And that was the end of the credit crisis.

When the tight-ass at Second New Haven saw that the full loan was paid by a competitor, he panicked, and set up a meeting with Frank and Walter to try and win back their business. The two listened patiently to the presentation, feigned interest and enthusiasm…and then Frank told them to pound sand.

I mention that story because it recalls the date he went on with his girlfriend Anna, after he found out about her exploits from the stranger on the plane. Remember? He took her dancing, flirted with her, led her to believe everything was wonderful—and then dropped the hammer. This is exactly what he did with the Second New Haven bankers (although that meeting was probably much less exciting than a night of lascivious dancing). Most people would not have wasted time or energy taking that meeting. Not Frank. As with his doomed girlfriend, he wanted them to know exactly what they'd be missing by betraying his trust.

32

HAPPY TRAILS

WHILE THE MANUFACTURING OF DENTAL ALLOYS may not sound like the most exciting business in the world, Jensen Industries was, by necessity, involved with the gold market. And the gold market is notorious for arousing the interest of all manner of colorful characters. Gold prospecting still happens in the modern era; it just takes on different forms. Otherwise sane people go stark, raving mad at the thought of gold. And Frank had to do business with some of those maniacs.

For one thing, the price of gold, as discussed, was prone to wild fluctuation. Jensen needed the stuff to make their alloys, but they still had to pay to acquire it—and the price was what the price was. As this chart shows, the late 70s/early 80s was one of the more volatile periods for gold prices:

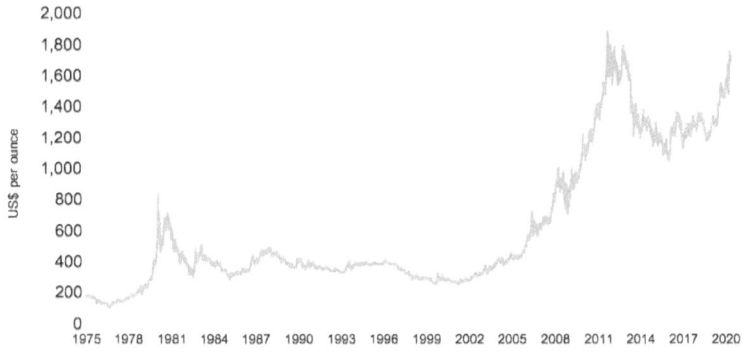

Bullion companies have elaborate methods of hedging, to avoid being caught if the price goes haywire. I once had dinner with a guy who dealt in gold bullion, and he explained to me exactly how they managed to buy and sell gold without risking their position. His method made perfect sense at the time—or maybe it was all the wine I drank—but it's a bit too fuzzy for me to grasp. Frank didn't want to waste time trying to game the system. The way he worked it was simple. "I made sure and bought exactly the same amount of gold every day that I'd sold the day before," he told me. That was an imperfect system, for sure—but he always increased the prices immediately, and was slow to lower them. Over the course of his time at Jensen, it worked more to his advantage than the other way around.

Even so, there were occasions when the gold price increased so rapidly that he was forced to be a trader, whether he wanted to or not. In one four-month period from 1979-80, the price of an ounce of gold rose from $300 to $800. Suddenly everyone and their grandmother was sending scrap batches in the mail. One customer with a paranoid bent showed up at the office with two armed guards, scaring the bejesus out of one of the new sales staffers, a normally unflappable single mother named Lorraine Borkowski.

There was an off-duty cop who showed up with a 55-gallon drum of liquid sludge that he claimed contained gold. Usually the gold being offered was more accessible, but Frank agreed to examine the sludge. Drawing on his Michigan Tech days, when he took a class on Electro-Metallurgy, he added zinc powder to the liquid.

"If you have a solution that contained gold," he explained, "in order to retrieve the gold, you have to add a metal that would tie up the negative ion, in this case chlorine. The heavier metal—gold, in this case—would precipitate from solution."

Presto, change-o, rearrange-o: gold!

He called the cop, whose name was Mike, and told him the good news. Three more times, Mike showed up with these mysterious drums of liquid sludge. Three more times, Frank did his alchemy with the zinc powder, isolating the gold.

But the fourth time Mike showed up with a drum, there was no gold in the sludge. His supplier had pulled a fast one. Frank never found out how that situation resolved itself, because that was the last time the cop came to the lab with a 55-gallon drum.

And then there was a business acquaintance of Frank's, a man named John Hoffman. He'd worked for both Jennifer and Jensen before relocating to Pennsylvania and setting up his own refining operation in the optimistically-named Happy Valley Farms. They were "friendly competitors," as Frank put it, who sometimes did a little business, usually involving palladium or platinum.

One day Hoffman called, and there was an evangelical zeal in his voice, as with the recently converted who have found Jesus or turned vegan. "I have the most amazing news," he said. "Inside information. The price of gold is going to go to $2,000 an ounce, and silver will go up to $100."

"John," Frank told him, "the first rule of the gold business is that no one knows anything about the price of gold."

"I'm telling you," he said, his voice pleading. "It's going up. Way up. You need to buy up all you can and hold on to it. Don't sell! If you do that, you'll be rich—rich, I tell you!"

After the call, Frank and Walter met to discuss what Hoffman had told them.

"He seems pretty convinced," Walter said.

"That doesn't mean he's right. How would he know?"

"But what if he *is* right?"

"Then good for him. We're in the dental alloy business, not the gold speculation business. Let's keep it that way."

This proved to be the right move. Soon after that call, the price of gold collapsed. The gold that poor Hoffman hoarded, for which he'd paid $800 an ounce, was now worth far less. He'd invested so much money, and the price had dropped so precipitously, that he couldn't service his debts. John Hoffman went broke, gold prospecting.

JENSEN INDUSTRIES OPENED ITS DOORS on April 1, 1976. Twelve years later, with no more worlds to conquer, Franklin was no longer jazzed about his day to day. Boredom set it. He began to spend less time at the office. He took longer summer trips back to Michigan to visit his sister. He traveled more.

In 1988, Jensen was visited by an up-and-comer named David Klein—young, handsome, charming, with piercing blue eyes and a wonderful bedside manner. "I liked him almost immediately," Frank recalled.

He was husky but carried it well. He wore nice clothes and drove a nice car. His wife was attractive and kind. He had five kids.

"Dave Klein was cool," Stephanie remembers. "He was younger than my parents, so he was into good music. He had a cool house, and they would play Cat Stevens records."

He was also a dynamic manager and a natural-born salesman. Frank recognized that Klein—who was not Jewish but of German descent, like the "paperclipped" Nazis at Lycoming—could be an effective general manager. So he decided to step away. He worked out a retirement deal that paid him $300,000 a year every year for ten years, plus any dividends from his share of ownership.

And on June 30, 1988, two days shy of his 50th birthday, he handed the proverbial car keys to Dave Klein. The man born in the house with no toilet in the farthest reaches of the Lower 48 was a retired self-made multi-millionaire.

But that moment was like when the price of gold was $800 an ounce. As Robert Frost wrote, nothing gold can stay.

PART FIVE

CHINA & BEYOND

Frank sports a beard and a Hawaiian shirt, ca. 2015.

33

THE AUTHOR APPEARS

WE ARE FAST APPROACHING the part of the story in which I appear—a part which now, because time is a rocket, spans 23 years. After a few months of courtship, Stephanie and I began dating in February of 2000, a few weeks after the Y2K disaster that wasn't. We moved in together that August, to a fifth-floor walk-up on East 7th Street in the East Village.

When I came into the picture, Stephanie was hosting a live AM radio show, "The Secrets of Health and Longevity," where her father, Dr. St. John, was the only guest. She didn't use her full name, I think to make it seem like she wasn't his daughter, and instead went by the very fake-sounding "Stephanie Marie."

The radio show was really an infomercial—the airtime was paid for by HerbaSway Laboratories, the Chinese herbal remedy company Franklin had founded a few years prior, when the boredom of retirement and the sudden loss of his beloved sister, Jeanie, lured him back into the work force. The company's flagship product was called HerbaGreen Tea. It was a green tea concentrate, a patented formula, touted to have enormous health benefits—which, if you read up on green tea, it absolutely did and does have.

At some point, the AM station was gobbled up by ESPN, and the radio show ended. After that, Stephanie had to drive periodically to Wallingford to record infomercials. These infomercials, the bread and butter of the company's marketing efforts, ran on AM stations all over the country.

When Frank first gave me a tour of the company's facilities—this was in 2000 or 2001—HerbaSway occupied two different buildings: a manufacturing plant, where the green tea concentrates were produced and put into the little glass bottles, and the administrative offices, which occupied a brick building in a tree-lined industrial office park, where the sales staff and everyone else were situated. He had a great big office, bigger than our current living/dining room, with a desk and chairs, an industrial sofa, and on the drab white walls, various UConn Women's Basketball posters in matted frames. He had his own "executive bathroom," which had no windows but a jet engine of a fan and a few bottles of some sort of concentrated fragrant spray.

The impression, as I walked around, was that he had just moved in a week ago. There wasn't a "lived in" feeling at all. Some of the framed posters had not yet been hung, and the vast office felt like much more space than was required.

In the warren of rooms that comprised the administrative offices was a soundproofed studio, where father and daughter would record the informercials. For a brief period, I took over the hosting duties—I called myself "Dave Goodman," which sounded like a trustworthy name—and I would alternate asking them questions about the various products.

From all indications, Frank seemed happy. He had a new company that sold products he zealously believed in. Lorraine, his second wife—the same Lorraine who was freaked out at Jensen Industries when the paranoid gold customer showed up with armed guards—was working there with him. And from what I could gather, the employees liked it well enough (although they would be pre-disposed to appear that way, knowing that I was the visiting son-in-law, a potential Gordon Katz to the whole operation, a stranger whose ass needed to be kissed). It was during one of those early visits that Frank got the check for a hundred fifty grand in the mail, where he did the little dance.

The mad scientist of HerbaSway was a Chinese-American named James Guo. A geneticist at Yale University in nearby New Haven, and an expert in Chinese herbal remedies, he was the one who came up with all the patented formulas that Stephanie and I pretended to marvel at during the infomercial sessions. Guo practiced *qi qong* and back in China had been raised by Taoist monks. Unfortunately, the monks did not teach him how not to be a crook.

But in my haste to interject myself into the proceedings, I've skipped ahead a few decades. Let us return to Wallingford in the go-go 1980s, when my wife was still a kid, Guo was still in China, and I was back in Jersey, roaming the halls of my junior school...

34

LORRAINE: AN INTRODUCTION

THE FORMER LORRAINE PIATROWSKI was born on September 5, 1943, in Salem, Mass. That seems like a mundane statement, but much can be gleaned from these simple facts. First, Lorraine, like Barbara, is of Polish ancestry. Second, she is five years younger than Frank. Third, she is a Virgo, and possessed of all the qualities for which that zodiac sign is known: neatness, punctuality, superb organizational skills, obsession with order. (That last quality was one my wife would sometimes run afoul of; Stephanie is also a Virgo, but for whatever reason does not share the same horoscopical attributes). Fourth, she is from Massachusetts, and has the accent to prove it—especially after a glass of wine.

What we can't glean from that sentence is that Lorraine is tough as nails. She emerged from a less-than-happy childhood and a failed first marriage to succeed in her professional life, on her own merits, using her own skill set, despite being a single mom. Whether she was selling Avon to Wallingford's women or metallurgical alloys to dental labs, she was pleasant, well-prepared, meticulous, and professional. What Frank saw in Lorraine was a woman who, unlike Barbara, had her shit together.

What Lorraine saw in him was a good father—the sort of man who, as a single mother, she was in the market for—who was also "handsome and a nice person," as she told me.

I asked her about his first impressions of Franklin. "He was saying how he was taking his daughter to see *Black Beauty*, the movie," she recalled. "I thought that that was a wonderful thing to do with her, which gave me good feelings."

Those good feelings dissipated almost immediately, however, when Frank told her the next day that he'd conked out as soon as the lights went down and slept through most of the picture. Even so, Lorraine decided to stick with him. "Little did I know that we would be married for 34 years."

Lorraine proved a wonderful complement to Frank. She took good care of him. She was fun-loving, excellent company, and loved to laugh. She accompanied him on many of his travels, as we shall see, and it was her friendliness and curiosity that attracted many of the people who would be important figures in the second half of Frank's life. It is no exaggeration to think about his life as having two distinct parts: before Lorraine, and after Lorraine. She was that influential to what he did, that important to him.

After Frank retired from Jensen Industries, flush with his golden parachute, the kids were at boarding school, or in the case of Lou, in college. With so much time on his hands, and so much money, Frank decided to travel the world. Lorraine was his companion on many of these travels.

In Egypt, they saw the pyramids and the Sphinx and the tomb of King Tut. Heeding the advice proffered by other Americans in that country—"Don't drink the water!"—Frank dutifully avoided drinking from a tap. Unfortunately, and much to his surprise, the milk he used in his cereal came not from a dairy cow but from a can of powder. The powder was mixed with water—water from the tap. So Frank came down with a horrible stomach bug that sidelined him for two days.

The second leg of that Middle Eastern sojourn took them to Jerusalem. "At that time, which was in 1982, Egypt was very dirty," Frank recalls. "So when we left for Israel, we were almost glad to get out of there. When we landed in Israel, it was like coming out of darkness into the light. The country was clean, and we were greeted by our driver in a Mercedes limousine."

Unfortunately, Lorraine must have had some of the reconstituted milk, because no sooner did they get to their Hoffa hotel room that she, too, fell ill. Frank wandered the ancient streets, taking in the sights, and brought her back a rose, which turned out to be fake. On the other hand, she still has that fake rose, whereas a real one would have disintegrated into the desert dust ages ago. When she was well enough to continue, the two of them made a tour of the country, spending time on a kibbutz. At the border, Franklin convinced the border guards—who were probably not much older than Lou—to let him touch his toe into Lebanon. Now he could say he'd been there, without having to actually brave the dangers of Beirut.

But the part of the country that made the most lasting impression on Frank was the Western Wall. The remains of the Second Temple built by Herod the Great and destroyed by the Romans in AD 66, the Wall is one of the holiest sights on earth. But he didn't see it that way. As he wrote in his memoirs, "In the crevices in the wall you can stick a note for your special intentions. Not to miss out on an economic opportunity, there were enterprising young people that for a fee would pray for your intentions. You could go on your merry way and have your intentions put before the Supreme Being. Nice job if you can get it. Anyway I thought it seemed as though it was a good con."

On another occasion, Frank and Lorraine went to Argentina—to fulfill his dream of visiting all the continents, and also to show off the Spanish language skills he'd recently acquired by listening to Berlitz tapes. By chance, they happened to make the acquaintance of an Iranian expat, a man named Ali Kai, a former official in the Shah's government. By the mid-80s, the Shah had been overthrown, and Ali had fled for his life.

He invited them to have dinner the following night at his estate in the suburbs. So Frank and Lorraine took a train and then a cab to this remote country house. If this were a movie, something awful would have happened. But because it was Frank, Ali wound up being as cool as he seemed, and they enjoyed a wonderful weekend with their host's extended family, all of whom spoke Farsi—a language Frank had never heard before. They so enjoyed each other's company that they met again a few months later, this time in Los Angeles, where Ali was going to visit his son.

When Frank and Lorraine finally tied the knot, in 1989, they honeymooned in that most romantic of cities—Paris. They happened to arrive in town the day the Louvre re-opened. So they stood in line and took in the works of art on display. They also toured the wine country and the battlefields of Normandy. That last stop was probably not high on Lorraine's list.

The most extravagant vacation was when they went to Italy: Pisa, Venice, Florence, Naples, and Rome. They hired a private driver and tour guide, who whisked them around the country and past the long lines at the museums. At the Vatican, they had a private showing of the Sistine Chapel. For ten days they were with the guide, "being pampered like you wouldn't believe," as Frank put it. The price tag for that trip came to more than $40,000—ten grand plus a sizable tip went to the driver. They paid for this up front, through their travel agent. Then a bill came in the mail, and Lorraine accidentally paid it a second time. "It was so good," Frank joked, "we paid twice!" The second payment was refunded, but he still gives her shit about it.

But the most famous trip, at least in family lore, is when he went to Antarctica. Because, again: he wanted to hit all the continents. When I asked him what it was like there, he answered with one word: "Cold." And this is a man who grew up in a house in the Upper Peninsula, with no insulation and no central heat—a millionaire who didn't bother putting a heater in the breezeway where he watched TV. So, yes: cold! "Third-class treatment for first-class payment" is how Frank describes the adventure.

The reason we know about his trip to Antarctica is because when he was there, in 1989, he met a burly Russian at a weather station, and gave the guy twenty bucks for one of those ridiculous but very warm Siberian fur hats, which, to this day, he wears all the time during the winter months.

Something else happened on the voyage to Antarctica. Frank, who was traveling solo—Lorraine wisely chose to sit out this particular trip—struck up a conversation with two fellow passengers. One of the women asked where he was from.

"L'Anse. A tiny town in the Upper Peninsula of Michigan."

The woman just about fell out of her chair. "L'Anse? Up near Houghton?"

"Yes."

"Do you know a man named Rick Moilenen?"

Frank did. Rick was a cousin of his high school girlfriend, Anna.

"He used to be my son-in-law."

This wasn't the life-changing random conversation with a stranger that he'd had years earlier, when the man on the plane revealed the hidden truth about that same high school girlfriend's alleged promiscuity. But it's still amazing that in this sparsely populated place, almost as far from L'Anse as it's possible to be, he managed to meet someone with a connection to his hometown. "I hate to say 'small world,'" Frank said, "but it really is a small world."

The trip to Antarctica changed him only insofar as it satisfied his yen to travel to places that were far away and cold. The journey that would inform the rest of his life is when he went to China. And that would never have happened without Lorraine.

35

THE PARENT SHUFFLE

I HAVE ALREADY PROVIDED THE SYNOPSIS of Frank's divorce from Barbara. But it was not a clean break. She was still the mother of his children, and their primary caregiver. She was also, once reality set in about the marital course she had chosen for herself, not thrilled about the prospect of staying divorced. Even though she was the one who ultimately initiated the proceedings, Frank brought her wishes to fruition. I'm not sure that she really understood what she was asking for, or what it would mean. She seemed genuinely to believe that even after the formal divorce, Frank would continue to be with her, just like he always had before, even during the rough patches of their relationship. Franklin has never been good about setting boundaries, but to his credit, he set a firm boundary with Barbara. Once the divorce was finalized, he was done.

When Frank and Barbara split up, Lou was almost 17, a boarding student at Choate, and more or less independent. Not quite 11, Stephanie still needed parental oversight. She went with her father to the "temporary" house in North Haven on Wednesday nights and on weekends; the rest of the time, she was in her old room in the house on Mansion Road.

The first time Frank arrived after the divorce to pick her up, Barbara came running out into the driveway.

"I talked to my brother," she said, meaning Walter, the attorney. "He said you're not giving me enough alimony!"

"And what did Walter say you should be getting?"

"Six hundred dollars more a month, he said."

"Fine." Frank took out his wallet, peeled off six crisp hundred-dollar bills, and handed them over. "I'll give you that much more every month. Now please get Stephanie."

On another occasion not long after, Barbara called him on the phone. "You need to come here."

"I'm not going to see you, Barbara. It's over."

"I mean it. You need to come here. I need to see you."

"No."

"If you don't come here, I'm going to kill myself."

Frank wasn't sure what to say to that—she very well might. Finally he managed: "If you do that, Barbara, then I get the children."

He called Stephanie the next morning, and could tell from the clatter in the kitchen that Barbara had not made good on her threat. He breathed a long sigh of relief.

Even so, things were not idyllic on Mansion Road. He found out from Stephanie that Barbara would often go out, leaving her home alone. That was bad enough, but then she met someone: a twentysomething lowlife by the name of Paul Bryant. The only time I saw him, Paul was decrepit, smelly, and toothless, but in the early 80s he was a handsome guy. He looked like he played bass in one of those cheesy 70s bands, .38 Special, maybe, or Bad Company. He was also a drug addict, who saw Barbara and her house and steady alimony checks as his meal ticket. He insinuated himself into her life and moved in with her.

Frank did some digging and determined that Paul was a drug abuser and, in his words, "not of good character"—an assessment that was borne out the year that Lou came home for Christmas and Paul tried to stab him with a steak knife.

"Barbara," Frank told her, "I can't have my teenage daughter living in a house with that strange man."

This set her off. "Then why don't you take custody of the kids?"

"I absolutely will."

"And another thing. I hate this house. You have so much money, why don't you buy it from me and move back here with Stephanie?"

Frank knew that with Barbara, when an offer like that was extended, it had to be pounced on right away. He arranged for a real estate broker to appraise the house, paid her fair market value for it, and had his lawyer make the arrangements to secure full custody.

This took time, and there was always the chance that Barbara might change her mind. When the judge asked her in court if she wanted to surrender custody, and she said yes, Frank breathed a sigh of relief.

As all this was going on, Frank and Lorraine were seriously dating—"going steady," in the old-fashioned way he put it in his memoirs. She had a place of her own, and a daughter of her own—Samantha, who was two years younger than Stephanie—and resisted the idea of getting married or of moving in together. But Frank convinced her that this was the right move.

Or maybe it was a tour of the Mansion Road house that did it. Barbara was never a neat freak, but any instinct she had about housekeeping went right out the window when Paul Bryant moved in. Stephanie would make a mess, Barbara would make a mess, Paul would make a mess, and no one would clean it up. The result was not pretty. Lorraine walked into the house and her Virgo instincts went into overdrive. She and Frank spent two full weekends deep-cleaning the premises, and by the time that arduous labor was done, Lorraine had relented and agreed to move in.

On paper, this made perfect sense. Why pay for two dwellings when you don't need to? There was plenty of room at the

Mansion Road house for an adult couple, two kids, a dog, three cats, and pair of pet rats (although Frank did make Barbara retrieve her two cats and gave the rats back to the pet store). Plus, he loved Lorraine and wanted to be with her all the time.

What he didn't consider was the effect this would have on Stephanie. At 11, she was living in the Mansion Road house with her biological parents and her brother. A year later, her brother was at school most of the time, and her father was gone, too, leaving her alone with her mother. Then the sleazy Paul Bryant moved in, occupying the same space recently vacated by her father. A few months later, her mother and Paul were both gone, the house was made immaculate, and the master bedroom was once again occupied by her father, this time with Lorraine instead of Barbara. And instead of Lou down the hall, there was Samantha, a girl she barely knew. What a whirlwind!

The only constant in this period was Stephanie herself—her and her cat, Rupert. To a 13-year-old, even one as emotionally mature as my wife, it must have been extremely confusing. That this all happened during middle school, always the worst of times for children, exacerbated matters. But my wife, to her credit, persevered to become a loving adult—and not only that, but to use her own experiences to help the clients she sees in her practice as a mental health counselor. Small wonder that she is so good working with teens!

36

IS THERE AN HONORARY DOCTOR IN THE·HOUSE?

MODERN PHILANTHROPY WAS INVENTED by John D. Rockefeller. If you think Jeff Bezos or Bill Gates is rich, they are absolute paupers next to Rockefeller, whose personal fortune amounted to three percent of the Gross Domestic Product of the United States in 1913. In today's dollars, that's something like $425 billion, which approaches *half a trillion*. That's real money!

Rockefeller was self-made. He understood that he had more money than he knew what to do with. He didn't want his kids to inherit every last dime (his brother, William, had no such reservations). In fact, as a father, he tried to prevent his children from understanding how rich he was, because he didn't want to spoil them. There is a famous story where his daughter went shopping for furniture at a store in New York. She asked for credit, to make her purchases. The shop owners asked who her father was, and when she told them—not yet understanding the currency of the name—they burst out laughing. Yes, they assured her, take whatever you want!

Rockefeller's vast wealth had bought him whatever he desired, but to his credit, he felt a civic responsibility to give a lot of the money away. And that was a problem. He was forever being accosted by con men, or cousins thrice removed hoping for a handout, or stray nuns asking for donations to this, that, or the other. It was exhausting, but it was also inefficient. And if there's one thing the great oil magnate despised, it was inefficiency. How to decide who should and should not get his money?

The solution was to professionalize philanthropy. Rockefeller set up a charitable foundation. Its job was to take his fortune and figure out how best to dole it out. Instead of handing out cash willy-nilly, the concern established systematic practices for doing so. His foundation invested heavily in medical research and outreach, and was instrumental in eradicating hookworm and yellow fever in the United States. Because of Rockefeller's innovation—and his money—philanthropy became a thing.

Franklin St. John's personal fortune vastly exceeded that of the average American, and yet it was orders of magnitude closer to the average American than to Rockefeller. But he had more money than he could ever spend on himself, and he enjoyed giving generously.

I have already mentioned several times him sending his sister ten grand in cash. There was also the time he bought his mother a new house. He'd offered to do that in 1978, when his father was alive. But Loosh would never allow it; he had too much pride. "I've lived in this house for 50 years, and by God, I'll die in that house!" Doris had no choice but to go along with her husband.

The following year, 1979, Frank arranged for his sisters to plan a pull-out-all-the-stops party in honor of his parents' fiftieth wedding anniversary. I've seen the professional photographs taken at the event. Loosh and Doris have grown old gracefully, and they look happy together. The party was fun—Stephanie remembers it being a blast. Frank watched his parents dance, and flashed on a memory of them doing just that at Beasley's, all those years ago.

Three weeks later, after Frank was back in Wallingford, he got a call from his father.

"I don't know, son," he said. "I just don't feel right. Something's off."

"Well, no one lives forever," Frank pointed out.

"Oh, I'm well aware. I'm just worried about your mother."

"You don't have to worry about her. I'll take care of her."

Loosh hung up. He went to the barbershop, got his hair trimmed, and hung out with some old friends. When he came home, he told his wife, "I don't think I'll be around that long."

"Don't be ridiculous," Doris said. "You'll live to be 90."

He didn't even live another 90 minutes. He went to the bedroom, closed his eyes for a nap, and never woke up.

Frank went home for the funeral. As soon as he walked through the door, Doris asked, "Is the offer to buy a new house still valid?"

Then Frank went into action. He called up Walter Seavoy, the L'Anse Street Commissioner and an old family friend, and asked about available properties. Seavoy knew a man who had bought two adjoining lots to build a house for his own mother, but she had retired to a nursing home. That same day, Frank closed on the transaction to buy the land. Within four months of making the initial request, Doris was living in a brand-spanking-new house.

"She was the happiest I'd ever seen her," he proudly recalled.

Frank has also been generous with other members of the family, including his children—and I'm no exception. I remember being at a diner when the kids were small—two years old and an infant. I was looking at our used Subaru Forrester in the parking lot, wondering if I'd made a mistake buying a car that had given me nothing but headaches. Within a week, Frank called Stephanie and told her he was going to buy her a new car! And unlike Dr. Katz, when Frank promised a car, he came through. I don't know what we would have done as a young family without his help. My children benefited enormously from his largesse, in ways they may never fully understand.

Frank also helped those he didn't know. As a beneficiary himself of scholarship money and the Michigan public school and university system, he is a big believer in education. He offered to help pay for the schooling of five of Lorraine's eight nieces and nephews, two of his own nieces and nephews, and children of his family and friends. When Louis was at Choate, one of his classmates, Tim Dibble, suddenly and unexpectedly lost his father, the breadwinner of the family. Although he had never met the boy—and still hasn't—Frank covered his costs for the last two years of his schooling. (Years later, Dibble paid it forward, establishing a scholarship at the school in Frank's name).

Through the years, Frank established and funded a number of scholarships. In 1978, he set up the Franklin M. St. John Scholarship at his alma mater, Michigan Tech, providing $1,000 a year for four years. The next year, he established four scholarships in the same amount at L'Anse High School. When his father died in 1979, he established a scholarship in *his* name in nearby Baraga, where Loosh was born. All of those provided $1,000 a year, and are funded forever. As his wealth grew, he increased the amount of the scholarships, pouring more and more into the funds.

His mother was active in the Catholic community in L'Anse. Every time he came home, at her request, he would make a donation. He bought a car for a nun. He paid to have the church kitchen renovated. On one occasion, Doris asked him to pay for a new roof for the Catholic school—a big expense.

When he and Lorraine met with the Sister who headed the school, he was surprised to see her wearing a fashionable black dress with a regular hemline, rather than the old garb he was used to seeing.

"Why Sister," he quipped, "I see you've got out of the habit."

She laughed politely. Then they talked about religion, and Frank, to Lorraine's chagrin, reminisced about his experiences in the church.

"We had to go to confession every month," he said. "The priest would make us tell him if we masturbated." He took off his glasses and held them up. "The priest said if I continued doing this, I'd go blind. I quit once I needed glasses."

Lorraine's face turned bright pink in embarrassment, but the nun laughed. And, as Frank put it, "She got her roof."

When his Doris died in 1988, Franklin donated $50,000 to set up a scholarship fund at the school.

Back in Connecticut, he's given $250,000 or more to the University of Connecticut, mostly because these donations buy him preferential seating at UConn basketball games. He watched both the men's and the women's teams, but it was the women, and their coach, Geno Auriemma, that he most enjoyed. And with good reason—right around the time he began following the team, the Huskies went on one of the greatest runs in the history of college sports. Among the players he met were Rebecca Lobo, Maya Moore, Sue Bird, and the greatest of them all, Diana Taurasi.

But his main contribution comprised two million-dollar CRUTs. That ugly acronym stands for Charitable Remainder Unit Trust. He set up the first one in 1999, and the second in 2011. The interest earned from these CRUTs funds the Franklin St. John Endowed Chair in the Metallurgy and Materials Department at Michigan Technological University. As a show of gratitude for his munificence, Michigan Tech awarded him an honorary doctorate. He is now *Dr.* St. John—a title that would serve him well in his next business venture, as we shall see.

37

DAVE KLEIN, SNAKE IN THE GRASS

I met Walter and Barbara Jensen a few times. They came to my wedding. He was tall, but stood sort of stooped over, to accommodate her short stature. They looked like a couple that belonged together. They looked close. They came to the reception, they had a good time, and they gave a generous gift.

I've never met Dave Klein. I've never even seen a picture of him. And I don't *have* a clear picture of him. Of all the important characters in the story of Franklin St. John's life, Dave Klein is the one I have the most trouble understanding. It makes sense to me why Gilson was petty, why Leon Katz had issues giving Frank his old Cadillac, why Walter Jensen was wishy-washy in matters of business. But I will never understand why Dave Klein—loyal husband, father of five, and a guy my wife remembers as being cool—stuck that knife in his benefactor Franklin's back.

Here's what happened: In 1991, three years after Frank retired from Jensen Industries, Dave Klein made it known that he wanted an ownership stake in the company. At the time, Frank was particularly flush with cash. Remember the small bank he'd loaned a quarter million dollars to, because it was on the brink of failure? He did that as a mitzvah, to give back to the people who had done right by him. He didn't really expect to see the money again. He assumed the preferred shares he'd purchased would wind up worthless. Instead, they increased in value more than three times in a few years. When he divested, his $250,000 became $800,000.

So he didn't need Dave Klein's money. But giving him a small ownership stake, Frank reasoned, would further incentivize Klein to maximize company earnings. And he was a younger man, with a house full of kids—he had enormous living expenses. Frank felt that making him buy the stock would put him in a financially precarious place. And he wanted to be generous, in a way that his mentor, Leon Katz, could never quite manage. So he and Walter decided to gift Klein three percent of Jensen Industries. What did it matter if Franklin owned 48.5 percent of the shares instead of 50?

As it happened, it mattered a great deal.

When he retired, Frank signed a ten-year contract, which paid him mid-six-figures every year, plus his share of the profits. As it happened, there was a clause in his contract stating that if Jensen Industries were sold, or merged, the terms of the agreement were null and void. In 1999, that dastardly snake Dave Klein began negotiating with a German company to merge with Jensen Industries. If that merger went through, Frank would be shit out of luck—or "SOOL," as he euphemistically put it in his memoir. Even though he owned 48.5 percent of the company, Walter's 48.5 percent combined with Dave Klein's three percent gave them controlling interest—by the 1.5 percent he'd relinquished gratis. If they decided to merge with the Germans, there wasn't a damned thing Frank could do about it. True, he'd still have a stake in the company, but who knows what that might look like, when the dust settled and the smoke cleared?

"Perhaps," Dave Klein suggested, "you might be willing to have the company buy out your shares?"

And so, after a period of back-and-forth negotiation, Frank received $6.7 million for his stake in Jensen Industries.

The company he founded with his old friend, that perfect alloy of the talents of two individuals—the company that made him rich beyond his wildest dreams—was taken away from him by a smooth-talking arriviste, who only had control *because it had been given to him*. For free. As a gift. And this was the thanks that Franklin got!

When Robert Trujillo joined Metallica in 2003, replacing estranged bassist Jason Newsted, the band gave him a check for a million dollars, as a show of their commitment to him. Trujillo did not then work with Lars Ulrich to kick James Hetfield out of the band—he was grateful for his good fortune, and has played bass happily for Metallica ever since.

My grandfather was born in the United States but grew up in Italy, moving back stateside when he was a teenager. When his cousins or other extended members of his family in the old country came over, he always helped them. He'd give them money, a place to stay, whatever they might need. Almost always, these cousins turned on him as soon as they found their footing. It was like the existence of my grandfather reminded them of their previous station as poor immigrants. Was there something of that in Dave Klein? Was he irked by the fat checks he had to sign every two weeks, made out to a guy who didn't even come to work anymore? Was he jealous, because he didn't create the company, just took over the operation of what was already a well-oiled money-making machine? Did he need more stuff than the ample stuff he already possessed? What was it?

Barbara Jensen, Walter's wife, had worked at the company since its inception. She was a secretary and kept the books. When she retired, Frank told me, she was being paid the same paltry salary she earned the day she started. And, sure, her husband was one of the owners, but if you're the great businessman like Dave Klein fancied himself to be, how do you not properly compensate your employees?

From what I can gather, Klein is a soulless jackal, concerned only with siring as many brats as he could spawn—you know, because his seed is so wonderful—listening to young-person music, cruising around in sports cars that he thinks make him seem cool but only call attention to his inadequate manhood, and screwing over his benefactors because he lacks the talent or ability to create anything valuable on his own. If he'd never met Franklin, he'd probably be trying to sell life insurance policies to the young and healthy. Klein is all about appearances: the blonde wife, the hip records, the Ralph Lauren shirt. But that shiny veneer barely conceals the ugly, vapid mountebank beneath.

The more urgent question is, why would Walter Jensen go along with such a scheme? Why would he agree to dick over his best friend and business partner? The answer, I think, is that Walter was a follower. As brilliant as he was at solving problems, at working in a lab, at navigating his sailboat, at building houses (he'd built his from scratch, by hand!), he was an introvert who was easily led and didn't like to rock the boat. Klein was a Svengali. He put the plan in motion, and Walter didn't have the internal fortitude to kill it. He just didn't have it in him. He couldn't marshal sufficient resistance. Always, he needed someone in his professional life to take command: first it was Leon Katz, then it was Frank, often it was his wife Barbara, and now it was Dave Klein.

Yes, there are worse things in life than being bought out of a company you co-founded, ten years into your cushy retirement, for over six and a half million bucks. But it wasn't about the money—it was about the betrayal. Frank had been screwed over by Dave Klein, whom he'd trusted enough to bring into the operation, and by one of his best friends. That stings.

Frank continued to see Walter socially. They had lunch at least once a month—as individuals, they still owned the building where Jensen Industries was headquartered, so they

were still business partners. Frank wanted to forgive him, and
Walter wanted to atone. But there was always an awkwardness
after that.

"I don't understand how you can keep seeing that guy,"
Lorraine said.

"It's like Dr. Katz used to say: business is business, and
friendship is friendship."

And to a certain degree, Frank could compartmentalize
enough to separate business from pleasure. He was able to have
lunch with Walter and more or less enjoy himself. Walter, for
his part, was likely relieved that his old friend continued to talk
to him at all—that there was no consequence for his own com-
plicity in the overthrow, other than probably a stern talking-to
by his wife, always a fan of Franklin St. John, and herself a victim of Klein's venal pettiness.

38

ORIENT EXPRESS

One day in the late summer of 1991, Lorraine and Samantha were riding the Amtrak back from New York. The conductor making his rounds asked if any passengers were going to Cheshire, a tony town not far from Wallingford.

"We live not far from there. Why do you ask?"

There was a passenger on the train, a teenager from Hong Kong, who was headed to Cheshire Academy, the prestigious boarding school there, and was in need of a ride. Lorraine poked her head above the seat and immediately spotted the girl. She pegged her, correctly, as a nice person, and recognized that she was a stranger in a strange land, lost. Asking for a ride while on board a commuter train to Connecticut was less dangerous than hitchhiking, but it was still a risk. So Lorraine walked over and said hello.

"I'm Lorraine, and this is my daughter, Samantha."

"I'm Serena."

They immediately hit it off, Lorraine and the 17-year-old Chinese girl she met on the train. She drove Serena to Cheshire Academy, and the two of them agreed to stay in touch. On the weekends, or during holiday breaks, Serena would go to Wallingford and stay with Frank and Lorraine. In time, she would become part of the family.

Because of her friendship with Serena, Lorraine became interested in China: the country, the culture, the religions, the Eastern medicine. In China, Serena suffered from discrimination because, first, she was a woman, and second, she was an albino. She had fair, sensitive skin, and weak eyes that peered between thick glasses. Her natural hair color was an almost-white blonde; her parents had insisted that she dye it black, to fit in.

Animated by this new ardor for the Orient, Lorraine attended a lecture given by a Ph.D. from Yale University, a geneticist named James Guo, who was, like Serena, Chinese. After taking in the lecture, she decided to give him a call, to pick his brain about Serena's condition. She discovered that, in addition to his work at Yale, he taught *qigong*, a system of body-posture and movement, breathing, and meditation popular in China that balances the "qi," or life energy.

All of this appealed to Lorraine, who has always been interested in Eastern medicine and alternative healing. She hired Guo to teach her *qigong*. And Franklin was also curious about the practice, as it fueled his spiritual side in a way that the Church of his youth had lately failed to do. Soon, Guo was coming to the Mansion Road house every week, giving the two of them *qigong* lessons. The three of them became fast friends.

Guo was bullish on the idea of Frank traveling to China. The government was always looking for Americans to give lectures about business practices, he told them. "I could arrange for a formal invitation," he promised.

By now, Frank had been all over the world, but he'd never been to China. So he agreed. And to make sure he could get around, he hired a linguist from Yale to teach him Mandarin.

None of this—the *qigong*, the friendship with Guo, the lectures in China—happens if Serena had taken the earlier train to Wallingford on her way to Cheshire Academy. Sometimes, it seems, things are meant to work out a certain way.

In May of 1993, Frank and Lorraine flew to China as guests of the government. He gave lectures in three cities: Beijing, ZhenGuo, and Guilin. His earnest attempt to speak

Mandarin—at one point he wrote Chinese script on the blackboard, to the collective amazement of the people in attendance—made him a big hit there. But he was nothing next to Lorraine. Pretty blonde American women are a rarity in China, especially in the smaller cities and outlying areas. When it was time for them to leave, Lorraine was bummed out. "Now I get to go back to being an ordinary person," she lamented.

Among the Chinese nationals they met on the trip was James Guo's brother, Jin. He lived in Guilin, and like Guo was into Chinese herbal medicine. It was at the dinner there that Frank ate scorpion.

"How does it taste?" I asked him.

"Oh, about the same as tarantula."

After the first tour of China, Frank would make half a dozen more trips to the East. In Hong Kong, they met Serena's parents, well-to-do industrialists who had them treated like royalty. With their guidance, and with help from their friend James Guo, Frank started several companies in China. None of them amounted to much, but he enjoyed the novelty of being an international businessman, and owning companies in a country on the other side of the world, an inscrutable place where few Americans were investing.

Ultimately, Frank determined that the way forward was not to export American ingenuity to China, but to import Chinese ingenuity to the United States—to found not an American-owned company in China, but a Chinese-influenced company here in the States. That company would be called HerbaSway.

And it would not have happened, had Lorraine driven to New York that day in 1991 instead of taking the train.

39

MAGIC & LOSS

FRANK WAS ENJOYING RETIREMENT. He watched a lot of sports: UConn Women's Basketball, UConn Men's Basketball, football, baseball (he remains a Detroit Tigers fan, but with no available regular broadcast in Connecticut, he watched the Yankees and rooted against them). He worked on himself, going to therapy and psychoanalysis, as well as the *qigong*. He delighted in his relationship with Lorraine, which after ten years still seemed as fresh as the day it began. And perhaps most of all, he got to spend a lot of time with his beloved sister, Jeanette.

I never had the pleasure of meeting her, but her approval rating in the family is extremely high. Stephanie loved her—she was funny, fun, an excellent cook, and generally a good egg. Lou, more careful about who he chose to show affection to, loved her, too—she was his godmother, and she doted on him.

After the death of their mother, Jeanette and her husband, Kenny, moved into the house that Franklin had built. Several times a year, Frank would drive to Michigan in whatever fast car he then owned, accumulating speeding tickets along the way, and spend a week or three with his sister and her family. Sometimes Lorraine came along, but usually he went solo. He went so often, he had a small addition put on the house—his own little wing. A far cry from the days of their childhood, when brother and sister had shared a bed! They liked to go to the local Indian casino and play cards.

In what he describes as "the most boring night of my life," they went to a local establishment called Big Buck's to play what Kenny called "Oh, Shit"—because after the winner shouted out "Bingo," everyone else muttered, "Oh, shit." Frank played high-stakes Bingo for three soporific hours and never tried his hand at it again.

Jeanette and Kenny would often accompany Frank on his travels. They were retired, too, and as he insisted on picking up the tab, why would they refuse? With his sister, they mostly went on cruises to Alaska and around the Caribbean.

"In March of 1989, I visited Antarctica and walked on a glacier, and in August of 1989, I walked on a glacier in Alaska. I thought it was a 'cool' experience," Frank jokes in his memoir. Then, in case you missed the joke: "Please catch the subtlety of the word *cool*."

Florida, particularly Longboat Key and the Sarasota area, was a favorite destination for Frank and Lorraine. From 1989 to 1995, they'd rent a nice place on the water there, and friends and family would come down to visit. Jeanette and Kenny had an RV they tooled around in, and by then, they were snow-birds, living in Florida half the year. So the winters down in the Sunshine State were another opportunity to get the St. John family together.

In April of 1995, Frank and Lorraine had left their rental house and were staying the night with Jeanette. He was in the living room with Kenny when he heard a scream from the kitchen—Lorraine had taken a nasty spill, and badly injured her shoulder, breaking it during the fall. She spent months after that in surgery and rehab.

Two weeks later, they were back in Connecticut. Lorraine was on the phone with Jeanette. Frank called out a "good night" to his sister and went to bed. He hadn't been asleep for more than an hour when Lorraine came in, her face pale. "Kenny," she said, handing him the phone.

"Jeanette's gone," Kenny told him. "She's gone."

"Gone? What do you mean, gone? Did she run off?"

"No, Frank. She's dead."

That night, in that hour while Frank was asleep, she'd suffered a massive, fatal heart attack. She'd been experiencing tightness in her chest, but she thought it was part of the bad cold she'd caught the week before. If she'd only gone to the hospital, he thought later, when she first had the chest pains… but there was nothing to be done about it now. His sister had gone to the sweet hereafter, leaving an emptiness in his life.

"The shock is still with me, 20 years later," he writes in his memoirs, "and I still miss her."

The services were held back in L'Anse, where Jeanette was laid to rest beside her mother and father, her paternal grandparents, and her long-dead little brother Louis Paul. At the wake, Lou, whose relationship with his father was rocky at the time, watched from the side, not daring to approach the body. At the funeral, Stephanie gave an impromptu, a cappella rendition of "Amazing Grace," the intensity and virtuosity of which surprised even her. It was a worthy send-off to a beloved relative.

When the funeral was over, and the body interred in the ground, Kenny came to Connecticut, where he stayed at the house on Mansion Road for seven weeks. He was a mess, and he needed time to grieve.

"We alternated on the meal schedule," Frank jokes. "One day Lorraine would make chicken, the next day Ken would make steak or fish, and on the third day, I made reservations."

By the time Kenny left for home, Frank had taken stock of his situation. He was through with retirement. The only thing that could possibly fill the void in his life left by Jeanette's death was to try his hand one more time as an entrepreneur. He decided to start a new business.

So he gave his friend James Guo a call.

40

SHANGHAI'D

WHEN HE FOUNDED JENSEN INDUSTRIES, Frank had to scrounge for investment capital. He sold a piece of real estate. He put a second mortgage on his house. Even when the company exceeded expectations, it was a bear to get a bank to extend the requisite credit, as we have seen.

With his second major company, HerbaSway Laboratories, there was no shortage of seed money. Ownership of the company was divided thus: 51 percent for Franklin, 19 percent for Lorraine, and the remaining 30 percent for Dr. Guo, whose knowledge of Chinese herbal medicine was so essential to the business. The LLC was formed in June of 1996, a year after Jeanette's passing.

Money was no object, but there were other difficulties. Guo worked at Yale during the day, so all the experimentation on the herbal formulae was done in the evening hours. Frank enjoyed this part of the process, as it harkened back to the days that he and Walter Jensen would sneak into the lab. As he recalls in his memoirs:

> We would weigh the dry extracts and heat a solution of distilled water and vegetable glycerin in a gallon beaker and slowly add the extracts to the solution. We maintained the heat until we were sure that everything was in solution. We now knew that we had the knowledge to make larger runs of product.

At Jensen, Frank knew exactly who to call to sell his product: dental labs. The product was manufactured for a niche market he'd spent years learning about. With HerbaSway, he didn't have that expertise. Was he selling retail or wholesale? To stores or individual customers? Was he private-labeling? There were a lot of questions to think through, a lot of data to gather.

That September, they exhibited the new HerbaSway products at EXPO East in Baltimore, with some success. Encouraged by the reception there, they made small batches of the nine products—most of them variations on the original green tea concentrate formula—bottled them, and labeled them with designs rendered by Lorraine and Guo.

And then, as he had with Jensen, Frank got lucky. A company in New York approached him to private-label the green tea concentrate, which they agreed to do. When sales to that one customer exploded, HerbaSway became a viable commercial concern. Frank had done it again! He'd captured lighting in a bottle—twice! Things were great for two years, until the company in New York found a cheaper supplier. Then it was back to square one.

The next breakthrough came on the radio, of all places. WEVD 1050 in New York, a 50,000-watt AM station, broadcast a health program, which invited Dr. Guo on as a guest. He has an interesting backstory, which played well on the radio. HerbaSway used it to great effect in its marketing materials and company literature. It goes like this (I'm quoting here from his current website, and will not fix any grammatical errors):

Dr. James Guo was born in China During the Cultural Revolution, [sic] his father, who was a court judge, was murdered by the Red Guard. He and his two brothers were smuggled out of the city and into the mountains, where he was raised being a little boy by Chinese Taoist Masters. From the first day in the mountains, he was exposed to herbs and methods for combining herbs. At the same time his training began in Kung Fu, Tai Qi, Acupuncture and Acupressure. Finally he was trained in Qi Gong. Traditional Chinese Herbal Medicine has been a part of his training throughout his life.

At the age of 10 he began to receive, on a part-time basis, a "normal" education. While attending school, he was required to work in the fields, which he did until the age of 15. At that time he was given the responsibility of running an entire farming community, raising grains, rice, and various herbs. At 18, he earned the opportunity to take a competitive examination for college entrance. He passed, entered college and received a B.S. degree in Agriculture. He continued on and earned an M.S in Plant Genetics. After receiving his Masters degree, he became director of a laboratory in genetic research at Beijing University of Agriculture, a position he held for two years.

Circumventing the system in China, Dr. Guo wrote directly to a number of American universities. He was accepted and given financial aid by Iowa State University, where be received a Ph.D. in Genetics and Biochemistry. After graduation, Dr. Guo accepted a position as a National Institute of Health Fellow at Yale University; a position he held for two years. He was then appointed to a position as faculty member in the Pharmacology Department at the Yale University School of Medicine. His Yale research resulted in important advancements in cancer treatment and antiviral drug development.

Dr Guo has lectured on various aspects of Traditional Chinese Medicine throughout the United States and European countries. He is a monthly contributor for Health

Supplement Retailer Magazine, frequently interviewed by major television and radio net works in US and in European countries. He hosts various radio programs across the country. His column, lectures and radio programs focus, and seek to educate the Western readers, on Traditional Chinese Herbal Medicine.

He has taught Tai Qi, Qi Gong, Kung Fu, and given seminars on Acupuncture and Acupressure. Dr. Guo continues to do research in herbal medicine with special emphasis on standardization of Chinese herbs and herbal formulas to improve the quality of herbal medicine. He holds numerous US Patents in biotechnology and in herbal medicine. He has developed and successfully marketed number of well-known brands in herbal medicine and nutritional markets in US, Europe, as well as Asian Pacific regions.

On the show, Guo gave out HerbaSway's toll-free number—and lo, people began to call in orders! And that was when Guo, with his clunky Chinese accent, was on the radio. When "Dr. Frank St. John" was the guest, the phones lit up even more. Frank writes in his memoir about being nervous about these radio appearances, but he has a lovely speaking voice that is perfect for the format. He doesn't sound sales-y, and you immediately trust him.

And he's smart, as we have seen. Once in the studio, he saw that other folks were there, recording infomercials. Why shouldn't HerbaSway do the same thing? He had the money to try it out, certainly. And it would be fun. All he needed to do was produce half an hour's worth of solid content. Fortunately, he did not have to look far to find the right person to work with him on this project.

When Stephanie went to Syracuse University to major in musical theater, he assumed that such a degree would never have a practical application. And now, suddenly, it did. Stephanie had the training to perform in an informercial. By this time, she was also living in New York, where the show would be recorded. She was working at a variety of ho-hum service industry jobs—Pomodoro, an Italian restaurant; The Bottom Line, a music venue—to finance her musical career (by then, she'd pivoted away from the "theater" part of her degree), and was enthusiastic about the opportunity to do creative work with her father.

The first stab at an informercial didn't have a script, just bullet points. It took 45 minutes to record, and ran 27 minutes. Frank arranged for a call center to answer the calls that he expected would come from the broadcast, training the in-bound sales staff on the benefits of green tea, how to set up automatic re-order, and so forth. He then hired brokers to place the informercial at various places around the country. The infomercial was a big hit, eventually playing at 150 radio stations all across the country.

Frank never let on that his "Dr." title derived from an honorary Ph.D. in metallurgy from Michigan Tech, and that he wouldn't even think to raise his hand if someone asked, "Is there a doctor in the house?" There was no reason to think otherwise, and anyway, he wasn't Clark Stanley hawking snake oil liniment. HerbaGreen Tea, the patented green tea concentrate concocted by Guo in his nighttime experiments, was and is great stuff. I'm not a health guy by any stretch of the imagination, but I take it on the regular and stand by it.

In addition to the recorded informercials, Frank and Stephanie did a live radio show on WVED called "The Secrets of Health & Longevity." It was a full hour, less the commercial breaks, and they did it three times a week. As great as meticulously scripted content can be, there is nothing quite like doing a live show when the audience can interact with you—I have some experience along these lines. First, the show itself is completely organic, and listeners respond to that. Second, when you're one of the live performers, you get a little buzz if you do a good show. Whether you're extolling the virtues of green tea (it combats the free radical cells that cause cancer!) or covering "Free Bird" at Madison Square Garden, the high is the same. Not only was he moving product because of the shows, but Frank was enjoying the rush of a quality live performance—*and* getting to spend time with his daughter.

On one occasion, Frank was set to do the show himself. It was playing in Chicago. But because of a time-zone mishap, there would be no call-ins. He had to do the entire hour show, by himself—without any preparation and without any callers! Most of us have had actual nightmares about a similar scenario. He grinned and bore it, and when he was done, plopped his head against the desk, exhausted.

Without the boost from the infomercials and the live radio show, HerbaSway might not have survived after the New York reseller pulled its sales. Instead, thanks to Stephanie and Frank's efforts, the company experienced its most profitable years during this period—the period when Yours Truly came into the picture.

At Jensen Industries, Dave Klein turned out to be a backbiting snake, ultimately forcing Frank out of his own business. At HerbaSway, James Guo turned out to be a no-good thief.

This is what happened: Guo had a connection with Celestial Seasonings, the tea company, which began to buy blackberry leaves from HerbaSway by the ton. Every year they placed one big purchase order, and then sent payment via check. (The check that made Franklin happy-dance in my presence was one of these Celestial Seasonings payments). In 2000, they found a cheaper supplier, but the order was so messed up that they returned in 2001. So the company was waiting for a check for $147,000.

Frank knew the head of the purchasing department at Celestial, and decided to ring her up to ask if the check had been cut. She said that it had, and they had overnighted it to Guo. A few days went by, and the $147,000 did not appear in the corporate account. Instead, Guo had made the deposit into a different account—one he'd set up for himself.

This duplicity wasn't a complete surprise. "He'd been acting a little squirrelly for the last six months or so," Frank recalled.

Guo was pressuring him to buy more *lo han guo*, an herb that is 250 times sweeter than sugar, which they used to sweeten all the products. But the company already had enough *lo han guo* to last for a few years. When Frank refused, Guo got angry. That response made Frank realize what was going on— Guo would have personally profited from such a sale, as the herbs came from his brother back in China. He was obviously strapped for cash, so decided to do a little embezzling.

Frank called the corporate attorney and the accountant, and when Guo came to work the next day, he fired him. Somehow, the accountant was able to get the Celestial Seasonings deposit transferred to the proper account.

That should have been the end of it. But Guo, being a mendacious little prick, filed a lawsuit against the company, suing for wrongful termination. Even though *he* tried to steal money!

That led to an expensive legal battle that dragged on for years, with depositions being taken on both sides. Frank refused to settle the case, on principle. Like Ulysses Grant, he knew he had more resources than Guo and would ultimately prevail. Also, I think he enjoyed sparring with the lawyers. He considered it a battle of wits. Reading over his snarky depositions, I almost feel bad for the attorneys.

What they learned during discovery is that Guo and his brother back in China had been drastically overcharging for the herbs—skimming off the top, basically. Frank estimated that HerbaSway lost a million dollars because of Guo's malfeasance.

After many months of legal limbo, the case finally made it to court. Guo took the stand and lied egregiously. In civil cases, Frank was surprised to learn, perjury doesn't result in criminal charges being filed—but it *does* result in losing. Which Guo did. The judge ruled against him, and in favor of Franklin. The lying thief had to pay the company $400,000—a hefty sum that more or less paid for the legal fees. The case was an enormous waste of time and money—Guo knew he was guilty, and should have just toddled off, lucky his 30 percent stake in the company was worth something. He tried to screw Frank over, but wound up screwing only himself.

"I am going to go to the great beyond," Frank writes in his memoir, "knowing that every business partner I ever had zapped me one way or the other."

But that's not entirely true.

After the Guo legal stuff, there was a period of great expense, when he hired a board of directors—Stephanie routinely described them as mobsters—who each took home some exorbitant amount of money. Frank also hired a succession of mediocre sales guys, each promising to deliver a home run, and each striking out looking. None of these people were stealing from him, or in any way dishonest, but they were a lousy investment of his rapidly depleting savings.

Fortunately, Frank was able to hire the one person in the known universe with both the skillset to run the company's books, and the loyalty to never even *think* of screwing him over: his son, Lou. I haven't written much about Lou in this book, I realize, but my brother-in-law is one of my favorite humans. He's smart, cool, very funny, and just a really good guy.

For years, the relationship between father and son was rocky. After taking 11 years to graduate from college—he attended a handful of them, including Syracuse, Boston University, and Northern Illinois, playing keyboards in a few bands along the way, before finally getting his degree at

DePaul—he wound up in Chicago, where he met and married my sister-in-law, Diane (whom I also adore). At the time, she was a professional photographer; she did work on various catalogs, including Crate & Barrel. He owned a sports bookstore near Wrigley Field—Lou is a huge sports fan, and used to have a service compiling fantasy baseball stats in the days before ubiquitous computers—and then worked as an accountant.

In 2005 or so, Frank made him an offer he couldn't refuse: relocate to Connecticut and help run the company. Much to our delight—selfishly, we wanted him and Diane and our niece and nephews within easy driving distance—Lou accepted the offer. He rolled up his sleeves and immediately went to work, cutting out waste here, downsizing operations there. Today, HerbaSway is a much smaller company, but runs like a well-oiled machine.

As for the disgraced Dr. Guo, when he left HerbaSway Laboratories, he founded his own Chinese herbal remedy company—much as Frank and Walter had left Jennifer to found his own dental alloy company. Guo's new company has a website that says, on the bottom, "copyright 2006," and may not have been updated since. When I called the toll-free number, I got a chipper woman who wanted to sell me a better warranty for my car.

And its tradename is—I shit you not—Heba Laboratories.

41

SISTER BARBARA

Stephanie and I got married on the first of June, 2002, at the Angel Orensanz Center in Lower Manhattan. It was a beautiful wedding, with some 160 guests, and we drank Dom Perignon out of lovely Swarovski crystal Champagne flutes that Lorraine gifted us. Franklin paid for the whole kit and kaboodle, and I shudder to think what the final tab must have come to.

At the time, he joked about someone mistaking him for a man named Richard.

"Are you Rich?"

"I used to be."

As if that wasn't enough, as a wedding gift, he bankrolled our honeymoon, a three-week trip through France and Italy. I'm not exactly revealing some arcane travel secret here, but I highly recommend both countries for your overseas vacation needs. Rome, in particular, is, as the kids say, lit.

Barbara was not invited to the wedding. By 2002, she was too much of a mess. Stephanie would have been worried about her mother the whole time, and she decided it just wasn't worth it. This was absolutely the right call, and I mention this detail because it illustrates how far gone Barbara was in what would be the last seven months of her life.

Later that summer, after our return from Europe, Stephanie was driving home from Wallingford, where she'd gone to work on an HerbaSway radio spot. Seeing the sign for Hamden, the town where Barbara lived, she felt a pang of guilt. She decided to call and check in on her mother. She was surprised when a man answered the phone.

"Hello?"

"I'm looking for Barbara. Who is this?"

"Who's this?"

"It's Stephanie. Her daughter."

"Oh, hi, Stephanie. It's Paul."

Why was the grifting loser Paul Bryant answering the phone at Barbara's apartment? Hadn't she gotten rid of him years ago?

The reason for his presence became evident. Barbara was unwell. She'd stopped drinking, Paul said, and this caused her health to fail. She was now at a hospital in New Haven.

"What?!? Why didn't anyone tell me?"

"Um…well…"

Paul wasn't going to say a word, because Barbara being in the hospital, paid for by the state, meant he could freeload in her apartment, eat her food, use her phone and her television, and hit up her ATM.

Over the next month, the picture became more clear. Barbara was indeed unwell, but not because she stopped drinking. She had colon cancer, it was advanced, and she didn't have much longer to live. Stephanie arranged for her to move to an assisted living center in New Haven. And one sunny day in late September, the three of us—me, Stephanie, and Franklin—went with a truck and a few movers to pack up Barbara's life and get her out of Hamden.

Stephanie and I were a little afraid, pulling up to the house. I'd never met Paul, and didn't know what to expect. Probably he'd be all bark, no bite, if indeed he barked at all. On the other hand, he *did* once pull a knife on Lou, and we were coming to take away his grifting livelihood. He had some incentive to be violent and angry. I was also afraid for Franklin—who, it must be said, didn't seem remotely concerned. What if Paul did something to him?

What I found instead was a tall man with long black hair pulled back in a messy ponytail. Much younger than Barbara, he looked older than Frank. He was missing a critical number of teeth, and his skin had that sick pallor of someone who has consumed far too much rotgut liquor. The apartment was a mess. Everything reeked of cigarette smoke. The curio cabinet, once white, was yellow—tobacco-stained by the decades of smoking. At the time, Barbara had a dog, a cute little terrier named Annabelle. We collected the dog and her things. We packed Barbara's stuff into boxes—her journals, her strange artworks, her knickknacks and family photographs.

In one of the bedrooms, we found the saddest thing of all: a girl, five or six years old, her hair messy, dirt, literal dirt, on her face. She looked like a street urchin from *Les Mis*.

Paul stood meekly by, watching. With Frank around, he knew who was boss.

We supervised the men packing the stuff into the van, where it went to a storage unit. We called CPS about the girl. And last but not least, we brought Annabelle to an animal shelter. As the tech walked her down the hall and into her new, happier life, we could see her body language change. She looked up at the tech as if she'd never been happier.

Between Paul, and the neglected little girl, and the poor dog, and the inherent pathos of watching movers pack up what little possessions Barbara owned, it was an emotionally draining day—more draining, in its way, then the day Barbara actually died.

By December, 2002, she had taken a turn for the worse. We went to see her in the hospital, and were shocked to find that her skin was now orange—her liver, apparently, was failing.

I called Louis, who was still living in Chicago, and told him that if he wanted to see his mother alive, he'd better get on a plane. So Louis flew out, and the three of us went to spend time with Barbara at the nursing facility, where she lit up cigarettes right near the oxygen tank in the corner of her little room. Barbara was, even at the end of her life, a funny person (as are both Louis and Stephanie). Somewhere I have a videotape of her cracking jokes, which decorum prevents me repeating here.

Even in her sickly state, Barbara thought of herself as the hottest woman in the world. When she walked the halls of the nursing facility, she acted like she was back at the dance where Franklin picked her up all those years ago. And she *did* attract gentlemen callers. It was nothing short of amazing.

Stephanie and I spent the last day of 2002 in Boston, ringing in the New Year with some friends. On the way back the next day, we decided to stop in New Haven, to check on Barbara. We found her back in the hospital, hooked up to some machines. There were tubes coming out of her mouth, and some sort of dark, viscous liquid in the tube. The doctor on call looked happy to see us. She was on life support, and he needed next of kin to authorize him to pull the plug.

They called for a priest. The one on call was a Filipino man, a gentle soul with a lovely accent and a reassuring manner. He gathered us round and asked that we pray for "Sister Barbara." Later, Stephanie would write a song with that as the title.

When my wife went to use the phone, I was alone with Barbara. I thanked her for giving me such a great daughter to be my wife. And I told her not to be afraid. But she looked afraid. She looked terrified. I don't think she really understood what was happening.

Stephanie called Louis and told him. She called her father and told him. "You could come here and say goodbye," she said. Franklin declined, just as he'd declined to visit her in the nursing home. He had no interest in seeing her again. He didn't need the closure. Maybe he didn't want to see her like that. Maybe he wanted to remember her as she used to be.

Once they shut off the machines, it was over very quickly. Early in the evening of New Year's Day, 2003, in the New Haven intensive care ward with her daughter and her son-in-law at her side, Barbara Powell passed away.

Two years ago, Stephanie bought for her father a subscription to Storyworth. Every week, he would be asked questions to respond to, with the goal of her learning more about his life. A recent question put to him was, "If you could thank anyone, who would you thank and why?"

Here is his response: "There many people that I could thank for many reasons. The person that I would thank most would be the mother of my children. The reason is that so much happiness has been bestowed upon me, because of them. My life would be so empty without them."

42

EULOGY FOR A METALLURGIST

WALTER JENSEN WAS A FEW MONTHS YOUNGER than Franklin, but he'd suffered for years from an array of health problems. By the end of 2019, he was living in a North Haven nursing home.

In February of 2020, he was among the first residents of Connecticut to contract the novel coronavirus—nursing homes were a Petri dish for covid-19, especially in the early days of the pandemic. He was 81 years old and already infirm. He didn't stand a chance.

Barbara Jensen called Frank and asked him to speak at the memorial service. He was reluctant at first, but not wanting to disappoint her, he agreed.

The memorial was held at a funeral home in North Haven. There were three dozen mourners in attendance: Barbara, their children and grandchildren, old friends. Frank only recognized one face from his days at Jensen Industries—the unfortunately-named Tony Scatino. Dave Klein, that despicable piece of shit, was nowhere to be found.

When the moment came, Frank stood at the front of the room and delivered his eulogy. He'd been considering what to say, but he didn't write anything out beforehand. He didn't even make notes. Like the time he had to do the full hour radio show by himself, he just opened his mouth and started talking.

"Walter was not a churchgoing man," he began, "but he was a good man."

And he told the story that I have chronicled here—how the two of them met, how they went into business together, how brilliant Walter was, what a good friend he'd been. As he spoke, as the words flowed out of him, Frank felt lighter, like a great weight had been lifted. Whatever resentment he may have harbored against Walter evaporated. His friend was at rest—a man he loved. That was all that mattered.

After, people came up to him, complimented his performance. He knew he had done his friend proud. And he felt that most marvelous of human emotions, which subtlety belies its psychological importance: closure.

Barbara Jensen told him something that was news to him: It was *her* idea for Walter to recruit him for Dr. Katz and Jennifer, all those years ago. "He didn't even think to ask. He figured you were happy down in Pennsylvania. I said, 'Go see him, Walt. You never know.'" She somehow knew that the two of them belonged together—and she was right.

Just nine months after burying her husband, Barbara Jensen died of cancer.

There is still one business that Frank shares with the estate of Walter Jensen—ownership of the building where Jensen Industries is located. In 2005 or so, Dave Klein offered them $800,000 for the place. Walter was inclined to accept, but Frank insisted they hold out. They were each getting $8,000 a month in rent, after all—why give that up?

In settling the estate in 2020, the property was appraised at $1.8 million—quite a bit more than Klein's offer. "If he wants to buy it, the price is $2.5 million," Frank told me.

I think he should hold out for more, and really gouge the little prick. After all, Jensen Industries has a refinery, which North Haven's new zoning laws prohibit. The only reason it can operate there is because it was grandfathered in. So the company can't *ever* move. Let them keep paying Frank and Walter for years after both of them are gone. There's some karma there.

Franklin has a blasé attitude toward death. "When I die, don't cry for me. I've had a good life."

He's said words to this effect so many times that I've lost count. He may even have said this the very first time I met him, at a brunch at Isabella's on the Upper West Side in the summer of 2000. That was 23 years ago. He was still in his sixties, his hair mostly the natural dark brown and not the Santa Claus white it would gradually become.

This year, Frank will turn 85. Although he is young at heart, he is by no objective measure young. It is the privilege of the young man—heck, it is the privilege of the middle-aged man—to forestall the contemplation of mortality. I can simply not think about my own death, because, while it may happen at any time, the likelihood is I have at least a few more solid decades left in me. At 85, it becomes an impossible subject to ignore. Death is all around, the natural order of things.

Most of the characters in this book are dead. Sam and Clara St. John, dead. Louis and Doris St. John, dead. Frank's sisters, Jeanette and LaVerne, dead. His brothers-in-law, also dead. His nephew, Jeanne's son Michael, dead of cancer at 50. The bosses at all his jobs in Michigan, dead. The pervert priests exiled to the Upper Peninsula, dead. His first love, Anna, dead. The Michigan Tech professors, dead. The Nazi engineers in Connecticut, dead. Slocumb, the crooked Midvale general manager, dead. Leon Katz, dead. Gordon Katz, dead. Walter Jensen, dead. Barbara Jensen dead. Paul Bryant, dead. Barbara Powell, dead.

Frank was blessed with a robust constitution. He's always been a stickler for exercise, and unlike other members of his family, he neither smoked nor drank (alcohol or coffee) nor did drugs of any kind. I mean, he didn't even take a Tylenol until he had shingles two years ago. He rarely gets sick, even with colds or flu, because he takes so many supplements. (The green tea concentrate really does work.)

But he did have a few scares. In 2006, he began to experience debilitating pain in his abdomen. He was in agony. "Lorraine thought I had Tourette's," he joked, "because of the words coming out of my mouth." He was seeing a naturopath at the time, but instead of sending him home with a fresh batch of herbs, she suggested he go to Yale and get an ultrasound. Initially, they feared his abdomen was laden with tumors, but it turns out that he had cysts on his liver. This was a genetic condition, something that he had no control over, but it would have been much worse had he been a drinker. He refused an x-ray, and he refused pain medication after the procedure. (He likes to boast of his adventures at the dentist when he refused Novocaine). But the surgeon removed a cyst that weighed a whopping eight and a half pounds! As soon as it was excised from his body, the pain vanished, and the digestive issues he'd always had when eating spicy food went away. "If what I had was, in fact, genetic," he wrote in his memoir, "then I feel sorry for some of my ancestors who probably died with this problem. Thank God for modern medicine."

A few years ago, we thought we were going to lose Frank. He was clearly in decline. He was fatigued, felt like crap overall, and his will to live seemed to be burning out. It turns out he had stage-four prostate cancer, which was misdiagnosed by the hack doctor he was seeing in the city. For years, nothing was done as the situation got worse, as his PSA levels climbed. Fortunately, before the cancer could do its dread work, he went to the celebrated cancer center in Philadelphia. Through a battery of drug chemotherapy treatments, the tumors were brought under control. He still has the cancer, but it is being managed. It is under control. If he is fatigued now, it is not because of the malady, but because he got tired. Certainly he doesn't *look* sick, or frail, or as old as he is. He still has a full head of silky white hair, and no one with hair like that can be too bad off.

I've lived a good life.

He certainly has.

As I see it, we all have an obligation to our God-given talents and to each other: to maximize the former for the benefit of the latter. We have a moral obligation to use what abilities we have for the greater good. There's no question that Franklin St. John has done this.

Think of all the individuals who benefited from his life's work: The soldiers in Vietnam whose helicopters weren't death-traps, because he figured out why the propellors were failing. The thousands of people who could afford necessary bridges and crowns that were not made of gold, or who benefited from the herbal remedies he manufactured. The hundreds of beneficiaries of his scholarships and other charitable work. Michigan Tech. UConn. The Catholic school in L'Anse. The dozens of workers he's employed over the years. And most of all, his family: his mother and father, his sisters, his nieces and nephews, his wives, his son and daughter and stepdaughter, his grandchildren—and, yes, his writerly son-in-law. Where would we all be without him?

Not much was expected of the fifth and final living baby delivered by Doris St. John in the house without a toilet a short walk from Lake Superior. But through natural industry, keen intellect, hard work, and, as the nun at Sacred Heart School might say, the grace of God, Frank has lived a full, generous, and important life. Yes, he made a lot of money. More importantly, he changed the world for the better.

We should all be so lucky.